TRULY RURAL, ADVENTURES IN GETTING BACK TO EARTH

Published @ 2017 Trieste Publishing Pty Ltd

ISBN 9780649725526

Truly Rural, Adventures in Getting Back to Earth by Richardson Wright

Edited by Trieste Publishing Pty Ltd.
 Cover @ 2017

www.triestepublishing.com

RICHARDSON WRIGHT

TRULY RURAL, ADVENTURES IN GETTING BACK TO EARTH

 Trieste

TRULY RURAL
ADVENTURES IN GETTING BACK
TO EARTH

TRULY
RURAL

By RICHARDSON
WRIGHT

HOUGHTON MIFFLIN COMPANY
BOSTON AND NEW YORK
1922

The Riverside Press
CAMBRIDGE . MASSACHUSETTS
PRINTED IN THE U . S . A

LOSE.

TO HER

ACKNOWLEDGMENT

Parts of this book having appeared in the *Atlantic Monthly*, *Vanity Fair*, *House and Garden*, the *Catholic World*, and the *Outlook*, I am obliged to the publishers of these magazines for permission to reproduce them here.

CONTENTS

TRULY RURAL

I

THE PLACE THAT WAS N'T WANTED

I

LIKE most people who do foolish things, we did it first and sought our justification afterward.

We did n't need a house in the country; that was the last thing we did need. The cook and the kitchenette cried aloud for a graduated family of aluminum pots, I simply had to have a set of Conrad, and she — she who requires many of them — needed several hats.

Also, we were bored. Any one who lives constantly in a big city becomes bored, bored with its straight streets and its scramble for precedence and the narrow circle of its parochial life. Our world lay between Fortieth Street and Fifty-Seventh, between Broadway and Madison Avenue, an area much smaller than Stamford, Connecticut, or Hollywood, California. People, too, had gotten on our nerves — endless strings of just people.

We were uneasy mentally. We wanted to get away, although our feelings had not yet registered the fact that clearly. Probably nostalgia is the word, the nostalgia a sailor feels when he is too long away from a ship. Not that it is the ship he wants, but the idea the ship connotes, the going from here to somewhere else. We wanted to go somewhere else, to get away from the overwhelmingness of This. Having attained That, we could, when we desired, come back to This again. Life would be a constant change, a flux.

Or perhaps it was n't nostalgia at all. It may have been the expiring ambition of a fatty degenerate frame. For, by having my world so circumscribed and by eating far more than was good for me, I had attained the girth of a tun, a sort of Gilbert Chesterton-Diamond Jim Brady corpulence. I had reached those proportions where, if cigar ashes fell on my waistcoat, I rid myself of them by the simple expedient of thwacking my sides.

Into this catalogue of miseries walked a friend, an old friend, fresh from the country. Prohibition having not yet darkened the land, we opened up a new bottle of that excellent (*hinc illæ lacrimæ*) "Vat 41." He drank joyously, and, as he drank, became loquacious. Finally he confided, apropos of nothing, "By the bye, I think the Farrs could be persuaded to sell their place. I've heard rumors to that effect."

"The lovely old Farr place!" she exclaimed — she, who is the light of my life and the delight of

my eyes. "That is the only place I've ever really
wanted to own." Then, turning to me, "You
remember the Farr place?"

I said I did, but it was n't the truth. I had n't
the slightest recollection of the Farr place. It was
just as if she had said, "You know, the Potala
Palace in Thibet?" I would have said "yes" to
that, too. On non-essentials I have always found
it the better part of marital wisdom to agree.

The next day we went up there.

So far as I could remember, this was the first
time I would set eyes on the Farr place. I may
have seen it once from a distance, but it had made
no impression. As we began to climb that steep
hill, I was conscious of exploring an unknown land
— a portly Cortes stumbling through the jungle
of real estate. The road was very muddy, I
remember, and the rain — for it poured —
dripped off the rim of my hat. Had it been winter,
I thought, the water would have frozen into icicles, which would have made a pretty design for
a hat such as she could wear to advantage.
Warm eyes shining behind crystal icicles dangling
from a wide brim. Charming!

A long pull, that road. Then at the hill's crest
we stood solitary and enraptured. There it lay
before us — the wide lawn with its broad herbaceous border, the meadow undulating gently down
to a brook, the farther reaches of an ancient apple

orchard, the promise of a huge cherry tree, the hilltop with its red barns, the roll of the road up to the skyline, and, nestled in the shoulder of the hill where the tall elms held their branches like umbrellas over its roof, the house. Severely classical that house, the dying gasp of an era of good, old-fashioned architecture.

My eye traced its lines critically. I would never be ashamed of living in it, the way I would blush to live in some of those suburban monstrosities, the sham Dutch Colonial, the bastard English, the unspeakable Italian.

Yes, it was good, and yet I had no especial desire to own it. For a matter of fact, I had n't any special desire at that time to own anything. Possessions hamper. I had been accustomed to going foot-free, to shed responsibilities like a bothersome coat. To-morrow I could pack my bag and go to the ends of the earth. I had done it once and I knew I could do it again. But if I had this . . .

Meanwhile she clung to my arm, muttering rhapsodies. "Think what we could do with it!"

I was unmoved, still pondering that hat with icicles.

"Please hold the umbrella straight," came the snort. "The rain is pouring down my neck."

That woke me up. I held the umbrella straight.

"Well, shall we go in?" I suggested.

II

It is not always an easy matter to look a man straight in the eye and say, "For so much money I shall buy your house." An artist can sell the picture he has painted and the poet his rhymes, but to exchange for gold the house a man has created seems somewhat unfair. It did then. I felt as though we were committing some strange and uncouth sacrilege. He had watched those elms grow to vastness. The soil had known his ministrations these many years. His hands had planted that border of flowers. He had given the place its loveliness, its charm of age, its atmosphere. He was part of it and it a part of him. Now he was very old — and we were offering him money for it.

He said he was surprised at our suggesting to buy the place; he had n't even thought of selling. As he said this, I saw his hand reach out to the wall beside him — a fine, old, gnarled hand — and stroke it, the way one touches something one loves very much and has loved for a long time. And I thought of what a woman once confided to me, the wreck of a woman of fine mind cast up on the lee shore of a London pub, how that she never left a house in which she had lived, happily or unhappily, without pressing her lips against the wall in farewell. "Something of those walls had entered into me," she explained, " and something of me into those walls. It is always like saying good-bye to part of myself."

The old man scratched his head meditatively and waited for us to make the offer. She — who is better at business than I — she said, womanwise, that we would be broken-hearted if we could not have the place. And she named the exact number of thousands of dollars we would gladly give to circumvent heart-break.

Hearing this he became suddenly alive. "Well," he remarked, "I'm glad people who will appreciate the place are going to have it." And we handed him a cheque to bind the bargain.

Then we went down the hill again, through the mud and torrential rain, she so happy that she did n't mind the water coursing down her neck. Nor did I care.

For there was running through my head this bothersome question: Now that you've got it, what are you going to do with it?

I could n't help wondering why people wanted to live in the country anyhow.

In some fashion I'd have to justify this magnificent gesture to my friends and relatives and soothe my conscience.

III

"Just why do people want to live in the country?" I asked myself.

"Well," myself replied, "because they want to escape the whirling vortex of a complicated city life."

"Stuff and nonsense!" I answered. "Country life is far more complicated — milking cows and tending your own furnace and all that."

"They want to sniff of its sweetness," myself persisted sentimentally, "and feel the pressure of its gentle winds on their cheeks. They want to touch the cleansing earth and taste of its fresh, untainted fruits. They want to go back there and get up a good sweat now and then, and feel the blood pulse along their arms. They want the sun to seep in through their pores and sweeten the sour spots Life's disappointments have made. They want . . ."

"Hold on!" I said to myself. "That's utter drivel! Too many people go back to the soil as though it were the cure-all for every misery in life. That's wrong. Don't make the mistake of thinking that the country makes for the simple life; country life is very complicated. It is much simpler to buy a bottle of milk than it is to milk a cow. It is simpler to run around to the grocery for a can of corn than it is to raise the corn on the stalk. It is simpler to let the janitor do it than to tend your own furnace. And as for flowers, the man in the city has only to stop at the florist's and buy almost any blossom he desires at any season of the year, whereas in the country he is obliged to wait for the season, carry on a guerilla warfare against pests, stand in constant terror of beating storms, and finally may find that the flower does n't come out the true color he desired."

At this juncture I remembered a little town in New England that, some years since, had been the center of a thriving Back-to-the-Land Movement. Young men and women with set faces went forth into the meadows. They took Art along with them, and its little sister Literature. They beat brass pots and printed precious poems on precious vellum. On moonlight nights they wandered through the fields feeling perfectly simple and reciting Keats. Then, gradually, Nature began to laugh at them — she usually does have the last laugh. By ones and twos they drifted back to the complicated cities whence they came. All that remains of that group to-day is a memory and a countryside littered with beaten brass pots and precious poems on vellum. The local tradesmen have set down the bills to profit and loss. Mention the simple life to a farmer thereabouts and he will expectorate viciously.

The trouble with these people was that they took to the country as a fad, and you simply can't take to the country as a fad.

But you can take to the country out of conviction (said I to myself), and people who go for that reason usually stay. Do not expect an infinite cure-all in country air and quiet, nor the solution for all Life's problems in hoeing the soil, but learn, by gradual contact with things of the country, that here are benefits no city can give, comforts no modern conveniences can altogether supply.

The curse of city life, I once read somewhere, is that it feeds so largely the surface emotions. We live superficially in our enjoyments and rarely are the deepest parts of our nature touched. The city breeds strange illusions that we often mistake for realities. It is difficult to keep city friendships. The city offers a competition based on material possessions and ruled by exacting modes that change from day to day. The forces of the city are forces of noise.

The beauty of country living (so I argued with myself) lies in the fact that it affords time and the receptive mind with which one can take his enjoyments to the full. Its solitudes give power to thought. In the country material possession loses some of its tyranny and exacting modes pale into the insignificance of silly whims. The material facts of the country have a way of changing into spiritual realities. "A landscape," as Amiel says, "represents a state of the soul." The country does not permit one to ignore the laws that govern the interior life, for the forces of the country are forces of silence — and the greatest forces in this world are the silent ones.

"Now," said I to myself, "in choosing between the city and the country you have to choose between two philosophies, between two ways of looking at life."

"Like choosing between a Dunhill pipe and a corncob," myself suggested.

"Precisely!" I replied. Which, of course, did n't mean anything at all. It was n't like choosing between a Dunhill and a corncob.[1] Corncobs are the sweetest pipes in the world and Dunhills the most expensive. But the argument had to stop because, by this time, we were almost to the foot of the hill.

II

THE AGE OF MIRACLES

I

WHEN we reached the bottom of the hill, being drenched, we halted under the shelter of a tree and looked at each other. The devastating thought struck our brains simultaneously: Where were we going to get the money to pay for that place?

For five years we had lived like the sparrow upon the housetop, which is to say that David's ornithological specimen lived upon a shoestring. Here were we, plunging into a financial abyss without the slightest hope of rescue. It looked as though there would be inscribed upon our tombs the epitaph: "They Bit Off More Than They Could Chew."

To this day I do not know how it was done. That is why I now believe in miracles. The natural order was set aside. The static laws of finance were completely disregarded. From out of nothing came something. The dead bank-book was raised to life. The dumb pay envelope spoke with gold. Yes, I do believe the water was changed to wine [2] (preferably Moulin à Vent or Château Yquem); yes, I do believe Joshua held up his hand like a traffic policeman and made the sun stand still. Did we not pay for that place?

The second miracle was marital.

Do not mistake me when I remark that the person to whom I have referred ecstatically as "she" has something of Nietzsche in her mental constitution. In "Der Antichrist," the mad philosopher has written, you will remember, "Happiness is the feeling that power increases — that resistance is being overcome." From the first day of our life together she appeared happy, and she had been growing happier ever since. Overcoming the resistance of domestics added perceptibly to her joy. Overcoming the resistance of new in-laws also added to her pleasure. Overcoming the resistance of erstwhile old girls was a distinct triumph. But the real pinnacle, the ultimate Woolworth Building of bliss was attained (to this I bear witness meekly) when she overcame the resistance of her husband. For five years of married life she enjoyed the sensation of her power increasing. The attainment of a place in the country gave her a new field to conquer. She could now heap Ossas of bliss upon Pelions of happiness. Imagine the prospect!

Then the miracle was wrought.

At dinner that night she looked across the table — she whose judgment I have learned to accept — and said offhandedly, "I'll tell you what!

When we fix up that place, I'll do the inside of the house and you can be responsible for the out-side."

Then I knew the age of miracles had begun again.

It began pell-mell. The carpenter who figured the new porch roof could be finished for $275, conjured up, apparently from nowhere, a bill for $1275. The stone mason and his assistants rode to and from work like Roman emperors, lordly in chariots of Mr. Ford's and Mr. Overland's manufacture. The painter wore a fur coat. A small boy to whom I offered twenty-five cents an hour to cut the grass scorned me the way that famous Tammany politician is said to have scorned a bribe, as being nowhere near his figure. All of these miracles I accepted with the rapture of the neophyte, and attained wisdom thereby.

II

ABOUT three or four times in life one happens up with occurrences that teach him a lesson, and the lesson is usually in fundamental things. Marriage, for example, or losing his job or having a baby or getting arrested. All of these prove that there are some things which it is not wise to enter upon lightly. So it is with acquiring a place in the country.

You become aware of a great responsibility

to that place, of a vast responsibility to one's neighbors who are sitting around wondering what you are going to do with it. They fervidly proclaim the hope that you won't do anything terrible — like putting in gilded Louis Seize furniture in a farmhouse parlor or planting magenta phlox next to red bee-balm — but in their heart of hearts hoping you will so that they can say as much.

The orbit of my responsibility being the exterior, I bent serious thought upon it. As originally built, the house was fashioned after the manner of a Greek temple. Then some early owner felt the urge for expansion and threw out a kitchen wing, which made the house lop-sided on the west. On the east the house rose sheer and abrupt from a bank. Obviously something was needed to dispel that abruptness, to lower that height, to make it sit down comfortably. In one of his delightful descriptions of New York, Henry James said that only one building on Fifth Avenue — the Public Library — appears to be sitting down. Now it is all right for an office building to stand up straight, long-limbed, and with its head in the heavens (business certainly needs to get into Heaven somehow!), but a country house should sit down, should lounge on its site the way an old man lounges in an easy-chair. Ours looked like a lazy fellow propped up in bed on an elbow.

Neighbors wagged their heads and sighed. They knew we would ruin the place. However, the bank was excavated and a red cement terrace laid with a low brick wall around it, and four square brick columns to support the roof. This was painted white to tie it to the house and the ceiling of the roof a sky blue, in the fashion of that locality. One must always make concessions to the architectural idiosyncrasies of his neighborhood. Trellises case in the columns and varieties of clematis spread their colors in great brilliant spots upon them — the cloudy paniculata in front, the velvety purple Jackmannii and the Duchess of Edinburgh's white on columns in the rear.

Having thus robbed this Greek temple of any Greek semblance, I then gave way to a mighty desire. I have always had a passion for little bay windows and here was the chance to satiate it. Inside, the hall was quite narrow. A bay window at the foot of the stairs would give it the appearance of being twice as wide. It would also make an excellent place for plants.

The carpenter said it could n't be done. A dear friend, whose opinion I value, intimated that I ought to be shot, putting a bay window on a Greek temple. "Damn the torpedoes!" I went ahead.

And there it is to-day, the first joy of our coming downstairs in the morning and the last at night.

Shelves are built along the back like the re-tables of an altar, where potted plants stand in seemly rows. English ivy has reached out its tendrils to cover the window frames, and creeps along the ceiling.

Since then the town has fairly broken out with bay windows.

III

ALL of this consorting with carpenters and masons and architects gave me a sensation of eminent respectability. Then and there I vowed that if ever I had time I would take up architecture as a hobby, as a gentleman's hobby. It used to be.

In the early days of this country no gentleman was worth the name unless he had a smattering of architecture, no gentleman's library was complete without its architectural books. Washington was said to have found time, in addition to being father of his country, to design a church, model a mantel, measure curtains and furniture for his house, and help lay out the Mount Vernon grounds. Jefferson drew up the plans for Monticello and was accounted one of the best gentleman designers of his time. Well, he had to do something to mitigate being a Democrat.[3]

In those days professional architects were as scarce as Egyptologists are to-day. Yet remarkably substantial buildings were erected, buildings that we are proud to preserve and copy as standard of their kind. It was classical architecture, to be sure, but it is not easy to be chaste, not even in architecture. It was built to accommodate the needs of generous, well-rounded lives — none of the present-day Puritanical sniveling and whining — lives full of good meals and lots of company and big-bellied punch-bowls and horseback riding and buzzing the girls. The men who designed and made our Georgian buildings understood life.

The native consciousness of our Colonial and post-Revolutionary builders, their knowledge of good line, good workmanship, and good materials, has not been exceeded since. One reason was that these early builders — what we would call "country carpenters" — had few books to work from and these were good.

I hold that the downfall of rural architecture was due to a plague of bad books and cheap designs circulated by manufacturing concerns and irresponsible magazines. My friend, Mr. Delano, the learned architect, holds that photography ruined it. When well-meaning people were shown photographs of the Taj Mahal, for example, they flew into rhapsodies and forthwith ordered the local carpenter to reproduce it in shingle or clapboard.

Well, there may be something to that. There's

no telling what a man will do after he has seen the Taj Mahal. But the fact remains that, despite our own architectural sins, despite our having led the country carpenter into the pitfall of doing the Taj Mahal in hand-split shingles, we still entertain the innocent notion that every carpenter who lives in the country is a master workman gifted with a native sense of design.

What a shattering of illusions when we meet up with him! Not that he can't hammer or saw or plane, but because he has n't a feeling for the materials he uses, has n't the slightest notion of scale, and his ignorance of detail is abysmally profound.

If ever I take up architecture as a gentleman's hobby, it will be in the same spirit that I once took up Anglo-Saxon — to read and appreciate poetic fragments — to recognize and be enraptured by bits of architectural detail, of which thus far, like the country carpenter, I am abysmally ignorant.

IV

MEANTIME, that is, while I was applying a bay window to a Greek temple, there was a great to-do inside — the slathering of plaster, the acrid stench of fresh paint, the swish of paper being put up, the curses of the carpenter trying to panel a morning room the walls of which were out

of plumb.⁴ It seemed to me that she — she who
knows an appalling lot about interior decoration
— ought to be making quite a pretty little home
of it.

One morning she came to me and seizing me by
the coat lapels said, "Carissimo" — she always
calls me "Carissimo" when she wants me to
agree with her — "Carissimo, I loathe Colonial
furniture."

"Well," I answered, "what do you want me to
do about it?"

"Tell me that I am right," she said, tugging at
the lapels. "I'm not going to put a single stick
of Colonial furniture in that house."

"Madame," I answered — I always address
her as "Madame" in my respectful moments —
"Madame, in comparison with your infallibility,
the Pope is a bush-leaguer."

So this was what she did, this miracle. I who
always believed that a woman should have a vote
now strongly protest that her place is in the home.
Before my very eyes I saw the vans disgorge load
upon load of furniture and precisely not the kind
of furniture I would have chosen for a Colonial
farmhouse.

"In the front is to be my morning room," ran
her edict. It had been the front parlor before.
"And behind that will be your study." Although
I had no notion of studying in there. "The cham-

ber at the head of the stairs shall be known as the Blue Room and the one beside that as the Yellow Room. Mine shall be the Apricot Room."

"And mine?" I asked meekly.

"Yours we will call Orphant Annie's — it contains only a cot. Is that enough, Carissimo?"

I agreed that it was.

V

A MORNING room, according to the learned authorities, is that chamber where the lady of the house sits of mornings to sew, interview her servants, and receive such of her friends as are privileged to call upon her when she is in négligée.

I had visions! I saw a bill for négligées coming in. I did n't mind the walls being expensively paneled and painted an Adam green, or the soft luscious green carpet, or the sea-green gauze curtains, or the desk painted with green and blue morning-glories, or the big barrel chair, or the chaise longue, or the William and Mary table, no, I did n't mind these; but an expensive range of négligées would have been too much. I had visions of her choosing an array to suit the background of that room — lavender and rose chiffon for Mondays, blue and pale green silk for Tuesday, a padded Chinese jacket embroidered with flowers for Wednesdays, for Thursdays cream crêpe bound with blue, Fridays penitential black expensively enriched with a henna lining, and Saturdays gay again with orange and quilted woolly white.

Imagine my surprise when I came in the first morning to find her sitting at the desk casting up household accounts in a pair of riding-breeches! The grocer's boy on one side, Mélaine, our blessed *bonne* on the other, and between them as chic a pair of doeskins as any costumier ever put out.

Since then I've lounged around the morning room in anything I pleased.

The study lies behind. Its windows face the orchard to the north and the stretch of meadow and the far-off hills to the east. It has every ear-tab of a study — shelves range down one side to the ceiling, built-in with cupboards beneath and a wide shelf to open books on. The desk is a long refectory table. Some day, when I have time, I am going into that room and study. At present I am concerned with filling the shelves.

"I wish we had n't given all those books to the Salvation Army," she said one day, looking at the gaping spaces. "Why not just put any old books up there?"

"Madame," I replied sternly, "there are n't any old books. I gave that set of Ridpath's 'Selection of the World's Best Speeches' to the Salvation Army because I thought it would save their cutting firewood."

That ended the argument. I have been left to fill those shelves as I think the shelves of a country-house library should be filled — novels in one section, poetry and drama in the second, nature and gardening books in the third, and in the fourth — more gardening books, preferably old gardening books with colored plates, such as the "Botanical Magazine" and Paxton's inimitable series.⁵ Some day, from the vast range of their wisdom, Dr. Eliot or old Dr. Christopher Morley may pick out the hundred best books for this purpose. Until that time I shall be content to choose my own.

Of Orphant Annie's room you have heard. It still contains the cot. A beneficent Providence and a tiny shop in Quebec conspired to furnish me with mulberry curtains and a bed cover at twenty-seven cents a yard. I have also acquired a sea chest, which is better than all the chifferoles, cabinets, closets, and bureaus in the world. Bureaus have drawers in which you are supposed to keep things orderly, but a sea chest, never!

At describing the Apricot Room and the Yellow and the Blue, my vocabulary balks. The Yellow Room, I know, has a mauve carpet and a yellow dressing-table and walnut beds with mauve bed covers; and the Blue Room is morning-glory blue — how else could it be? — and the Apricot Room contains, among other wonderful furnishings, a folding dressing-table with an assortment of unguents, powders, and scents that would have made Madame Récamier pale with envy.

Why all these cosmetics in the country?

Why, if you are asking me, riding-breeches in a morning room?

I cannot answer. I only accept and believe. Nothing can amaze me. All things are possible, and the more impossible they are, the easier I accept them. Tertullian was right: "Credo quia impossibile." I believe because it is impossible. I had not believed it possible to furnish a Colonial Greek temple without Colonial furniture. It has been done. I had not believed it possible for me to become a member of the landed gentry — I who was born a denizen of city streets. Now — unless my faith is utterly vain — I am one!

III

A MEMBER OF THE LANDED GENTRY

THE idea has got abroad that all a man does to become a member of the landed gentry is to buy a lot. This is a plebeian fallacy. The initiation into the landed gentry (I speak as one in authority, not as the scribes) is a long and complicated process. It includes a course in law, a course in finance, a course in the dialects of tax collectors, plumbers, carpenters, and bricklayers. When one finishes with it, he is an all-around, or, to use the vernacular, a solid citizen.

The landed gentry are divided into two sects — the Mortgagers and No-Mortgagers.

The No-Mortgagers are a dour, conscientious, Puritan lot, whose principal dogma is to own a thing outright, pay for it from the front gate to the back fence. They give as their excuse for this wild financial plunge the explanation that you are then paying interest to yourself.

With equal fervor the Mortgagers (a merry, light-hearted crew to which I am proud to belong) quote their article of faith, which says that paying interest to some one else is "good business."

The difference between these two schools is

that one pays one's self imaginary interest; the other pays some one else actual interest. The No-Mortgagers are solemn because, although a man may conceivably live without actual interest, he cannot conceivably live on imaginary interest.

Not until I became a member of the landed gentry did I know what interest was. It appears to be a sort of invisible energy — like blue rays or gravitation — that is constantly at work, and which one must check up now and again, the way he reads his gas meter. You must not pay $5000 for a lot without figuring a loss of interest on that $5000. (An efficiency expert friend explained all this to me, so I know.) You can't measure it in good health or sunsets or domestic pride or the valley mists at dawn or flowers blossoming along the garden path. Those things are n't interest; $300 per annum is interest. Do you understand? Money is energy, but a house and garden are not. And don't make the mistake of sentimentalizing over it or your account-books will be in a frightful muddle.

"Just imagine," this friend said to me, "trying to put down a sunset!"

To which I replied: "That's exactly the only sort of thing I can put down." And I showed him my balance-sheet with the items set down in orderly columns.

8– 5. One sunset with purple rifts and gold rims.

9–23. The first cosmos at the end of the long border.

10–10. Got a good sweat cutting the grass for the last time.

11– 8. A flight of wild geese going southward across a mackerel sky.

12– 2. An open fire, mulled cider, and a new volume of Neil Lyons.

3–10. The first crocus behind the studio.

3–11. The second crocus.

Thinking me utterly mad, he snatched up his hat and departed. And so I entered into the landed gentry an innocent.

You can always tell a new member of the landed gentry by these three infallible signs:

(1) His acquaintance with land values.

(2) His insidious hospitality.

(3) His refusal to leave his estate.

You are sitting — let's say, at a round table in a club — discussing with the men about you the relative value of home brews or the present Administration, when there comes a lull in the conversation, and a voice, apropos of absolutely nothing, will remark: "By the way, d' you know that real estate values are jumping by leaps and bounds in ——?" And he will name a place that sounds not unlike a Pullman car or an Italian dessert. That man — you can wager your last dollar on it — has just bought a house and lands in the suburb that sounds like a Pullman. It is as inevitable as to-morrow's breakfast: let a man become a member of the landed gentry, he will boast of the rising values of the lands contiguous to his. This, I say, is the first evidence.

The second sign is his insidious hospitality.

Having purchased a house in the country, the first thing a man does is to rush off and buy a guest-book. He enters upon a sort of Boniface phase and insists on keeping a record of those who sleep under his roof.

I have often wondered what eventually becomes of these guest-books. Quite an entertaining little *causerie* could be written on them. They are a pregnant topic for speculation. (I know of a man in Michigan who used his guest-book for a year, and then, tiring of the game, filled in the remaining pages with stories — good stories — that he read when you came to dinner. It was the only . guest-book that did n't fill me with terror.)

Insidious hospitality, I have called it; and the word is justified. He invites you up for a weekend, expansively telling you of that room especially reserved against your coming. Without suspecting him of ulterior motives, you accept. After dinner the first night, when comfort is beginning to settle itself softly upon you, your host will suddenly spring up, as if the thought had just occurred to him, with a "Oh, Molly, bring the guest-book. Jim ought to write something in it!"

For a matter of fact, your host has been thinking of that guest-book ever since you arrived. He has been waiting for a chance to spring it on you. Being a gentleman, you entertain the idea enthusiastically, and the huge tome is laid out across your knees and you are bade to "write something funny in it." You scratch your head, protest that you really have n't a funny tissue in your entire make-up, that your grandmother lived and died with a scowl on her face, and finally sign your name to a simpering phrase that in years to come you will blush to own.

The guest-book episode over, your new member of the landed gentry will fling another log on the fire, straddle the hearth in a proprietary fashion, as they do in novels, and, looking you in the face, ask, "What name do you suggest for this place?"[6]

There's a stumper for you! You wonder why a place should have a name, anyhow. You inwardly curse the idea of a name. Your mind goes utterly blank. "We thought of" — and he will reel off a series of picturesque phrases that leave you cold. If you are a brave soul, you may per-

chance suggest his taking the first three syllables
of his wife's unmarried name and coining a Welsh
word. But, whatever you suggest, whether it is
applicable or not, he'll finally say, "Well, after
all, there isn't any ·rush about it," — and you
settle back in your chair, thankful that the ordeal
is over.

But the crowning episode of his insidious hospitality comes the next morning. You appear at
breakfast in your best country togs, to find the
incipient member of the landed gentry dressed
in his shabbiest. "I thought you'd like to watch
me transplant some cedars in the garden," he
says merrily. You naturally offer to help, but
make a reservation on account of your clothes.
Whereupon you are assured that he can fix you
up. It seems that the incipient country gentleman keeps a wardrobe of old clothes of all sizes.
Where he gets them from Heaven alone knows.
But it never fails. Thick or thin, short or tall, he
can always "fix you up." And he does. You return to the city from his insidious hospitality
aching in every muscle, blushing with the memory of what you wrote in that guest-book, your
head a maelstrom of insipid names for country
places.

The third and final sign of one who has just
become a member of the landed gentry is his
refusal to leave his estate. The new owner is

always completely engrossed with the cosmos
bounded by his property lines. Nothing that happens outside them can have the slightest meaning
to him.

To these might be added a fourth indication
of the beginning country gentleman — his style
of clothes. Immediately after having bought a
guest-book your country gentleman will also buy
knickerbockers. He likes to visualize himself as
a sort of Duke of Abercrombie & Fitch. If you
chance to meet him wearing them, he explains
how much more comfortable they are for working
about the place than long trousers. Meet him a
year or so later, and he 'll be wearing a pair of
khaki pants.

II

THE novitiate into the landed gentry may last
six months, it may last a year. Then, gradually,
the country gentleman acquires a reputation as an
excellent diner-out — just the sort of chap to give
sparkle to a table. Then, gradually, the guest-
book is taken down fewer and fewer times, until
finally it is left to gather dust on a bottom shelf.
Then the place, so long nameless, satisfies itself
with a Rural Free Delivery number. Then
guests who come up are not asked to work, but
are told to amuse themselves.

There are those who say that when the country

gentleman reaches this pass, he lays aside the ledgers of the sunsets and his pen moves only to figure interest at six per cent per annum. This is a miserable fallacy. It is also a great injustice. For there are country gentlemen and country gentlemen, just as there are parsons and parsons.

(These things I have learned and I know they are the very soul of truth.)

There are members of the landed gentry who are satisfied if life pays them six per cent. These soon tire of the country.

There are others who are not satisfied unless they are drawing one hundred per cent. These never tire.

The one balances his books with figures, the other with flowers.

He who would keep the innocence of the incipient landed gentry never forgets that figures bear false witness.

For something must be charged off against horizons and green meadows, against the baked warmth of noonday and the cool of rain, against sunsets and drifting clouds and the wind through the cedars.

What is six per cent compared to these?

IV

INCLUDING THE SCANDINAVIAN

I

IN the pleasantly cautious phraseology of Connecticut law, the place is seven acres "more or less."

I'm sure that I would n't know what to do with it if it were more, and I hope it will never be less, for it would be quite tragic to wake up some morning and find that it had shrunk.

The line runs, so the deed informs me, from a dead chestnut to a point in a meadow and from that point in a meadow along several stone walls to a fence and along that fence to a road and by the road — the steep hill road — back to the dead chestnut again. If in a rash moment I should cut down that chestnut, or if "an act of God," as the insurance policies piously put it, should obliterate that tree, my property would be suspended in mid-air, like a man dangling over a precipice. The idea is too awful to contemplate. For fifty years that dead chestnut has held down its job — worse than the court clerks you find doddering around our sacred precincts of justice. Not a sign of life in either one. Being dead they yet liveth.

Fortunately, like the court clerk, the chestnut is amply protected; it stands in the shelter of a barn. And the barn crowns the hill; which, of course, marks the acumen of the man who built it.

Take any steep hill, and the problem of building a barn is simple — you excavate enough for the stall floor and put your hay floor on the upper level, which is reached by a road that climbs the hill around the barn. If you then attach sheds at right angles to this barn, you have two sides of a quadrangle. And if you want a carriage house, you place that facing the barn on the other side. Thus your barnyard is enclosed, and thus is ours. A drive separates the house from this group. To show their class distinction, the house and the carriage building are painted white; the barns and sheds have to content themselves with a dull red.

I could write many pages on the checkered career of that carriage house. We do not call it such, in fact, I've been forbidden to. Between ourselves and among friends it is called the Studio, which is quite a highfalutin name and gives the impression that one or both of us secretly practice some branch of the seven arts within the walls of that delightful little building. But it did start in life as a carriage house, and I'm going to stick to it. Its second blooming was as a barber shop — a former tenant, I surmise, suffered from the ton-

sorial complex. In its third era it served as a
gardener's cottage. The fourth was a studio, a
real studio, and to prove the fact there is the great
north light and the door on which an entire generation of artists wiped their brushes. A fantastic
door, this, more wonderful than any Cézanne.
The fifth period — we are getting warmer! —
saw it occupied by the cook. In the sixth — here
we are! — it becomes a guest-house.

Little green shutters and a front stoop now give
it character; hollyhocks range down one wall and
clematis paniculata struggles up a lattice by the
north light. Inside it looks quite cheery with its
dotted Swiss curtains and painted furniture.

I had hopes (I mention this fact unashamedly)
of making that building my Hoochery, where we
would brew the weekly beer and make casks of
cherry wine and hard cider. But Mr. Volstead
thought otherwise.

It is a crying shame that the Puritans have so
set their heart on the abolition of home brew.[7]
It was our greatest promise for the restoration of
home industries, and through them the restoration of American domestic life as it once flourished. Machinery has robbed the home of most of
its crafts; nothing is made there any longer; even
jellies and preserves are bought because they are
a bother to put up. Prohibition could have restored one of these industries to the American

home. Did I not have the pleasant dream of her lording it over crocks of home brew? She'd make a charming picture in dainty gingham sniffing the malt and watching the hops boil. Then, too, I had planned wine-making parties when our friends and neighbors would foregather to attend on the baptism of the infant Bacchus in dandelion wine and the sweet syrup of the elder. This realization has been taken from me; it is a great pity. Damn the Prohibitionists!

II

SINCE it has become the smart thing to have one's country place photographed from the air, I might persuade an aerial photographer to fly over here, for I've never been able to get the angel's viewpoint of my place. I have climbed the highest elm, much to the consternation of my neighbors, and once I essayed the ridge-pole of the barn, much to hers, but I cannot somehow succeed. Perhaps it might be done in this fashion — we might procure a number of those toy balloons so beloved of children. These she could — for she is uncommonly nimble with her fingers — affix around my waist. A man of my girth could accommodate quite a lot of balloons. At a signal she could let go and I would float heavenward — over the roofs and the tree-tops and the gardens. Then, when I had seen all I wished to see, I would prick the balloons one by one and be wafted gently to earth. This would give the neighbors something to talk about and furnish me with that comprehensive view of the establishment which only the birds and St. Peter at present command.

Let me say that my motive is of a solemn and sensible character. The average owner of a place in the country rarely realizes that, to develop it to the full, he should have a view of the entire place. That is the basic principle on which the landscape architect works. Lucky fellow, he has the capacity for tying imaginary balloons around his mental waist and soaring aloft. When he comes down to earth again, he makes the most enchanting pictures of what the place is going to look like after he has finished spending half a million or so for the owner. Well, a man with that gift ought to command big fees.

Lacking balloons I am obliged to survey this estate of seven acres more or less from the level of the eye, and remembering what it was when first we climbed the hill, I am content to say that it is good.

The lawn rises by a gentle slope from the roadway. This is very American and very rural. An Englishman would doubtless have built a wall there, but when I garden I like to garden *coram populo*. I like also to hear the remarks of passers-by, to see them stop their cars and gaze

over the velvet stretch of lawn and along the
wide perennial border to the little formal garden
of cedars at the other end.

A stone wall holds up this lawn and prevents
it from slipping down into the meadow. It also
gives us a level *tapis vert* which, measured in human effort, is three hundred perspiring paces
behind a lawnmower long and fifty of them wide.
It is precisely the same distance with a heavy
roller, only here the paces are measured in groans.

A perennial border runs alongside this lawn to
the depth of about eight feet. It is finally lost
in the farther reaches of the orchard, losing its
identity in the planting of cedars which walls in
a formal garden.

Another stretch of lawn lies behind the house,
a little square table of green between my study
porch and the rollicking bank of tall grass where,
in spring-time, the narcissi make of it a Milky
Way. Then the old orchard, veteran apple trees
with some youngsters started in to take the place
of their fallen elders.

With each lift of grade is a stone wall. And the
next grade up you come to the level of the barn
where the land on top of the ridge is fairly flat,
giving room for a generous kitchen garden, small
nursery, seed-beds, and a garden of annuals for
cutting. A few steps beyond that you come to the
imaginary line that lies between the heart of the

dead chestnut and the point in the meadow. Here order "bleeds off" into the tangled disorder of high grass.

Standing on the roadway before the barn under the shadow of the rose arbor that marks the entrance to the kitchen garden, the eye travels by sloping grades across two stone walls to the meadow, and beyond the meadow to a little brook hid in an alley of old trees. Recently a neighbor has dammed his meadow to the north and made an ice pond. To him I am eternally grateful, for my gardens needed the blue stretch of water to look upon.

While seven acres more or less are a mere gesture in land, I find that I never set foot in them but I discover some new hidden beauty, hear some new music, find my eye delighted with some new prospect. At first it was daytime exploration; of late I've been given to prowling around at night. Beat the bounds of your property at midnight when the moon and all the stars are out. A lovely patina of silver lies across the lawn. The borders become animated into a shrouded line. The vegetable rows blend one into another. And all the night sings to you. Sit you in the shadow of your arbor and listen. Music you will never hear by day comes to you on the night wind — the conversation of crickets, the rustling of birds, the far-off howl of a dog, the whistle of a lad going home through the darkness, the long, low hoot of a motor horn.

Prevented from seeing my seven acres more or less as an angel, I revel in seeing them as a bat. That is the only thing I have in common with the bat; otherwise we are sworn enemies.

III

"How much land is enough?"

This stumper she put up to me — she who has a genius for stumpers — one day when, in a profligate mood, she threatened to buy another meadow.

I replied that William Butler Yates would be satisfied with room for nine bean-poles, but then he was a bean-pole sort of person, anyway; I think I also quoted Horace at her and something from Lacordaire.[8] She replied that I was a fool for talking highbrow, which I doubtless was, and insisted on discussing this matter seriously.

"But why seriously?" I protested.

"Because you are getting too thin."

I pondered this reply for a moment and then glanced down my contour. Something was missing! I had lost my ample curve! I, who always carried a walking-stick because it gave my appearance a very needed straight line, now was an aggregation of straight lines. It was an appalling realization.

"Yes, it is true," I murmured solemnly.

"I was just thinking," she replied, "that if you lose thirty pounds tending to seven acres, what would become of you if you have three more."

"Madame," I addressed her, making the awkward bow characteristic of painfully thin men, "you have answered your own question. Seven acres more or less are enough for any man. Beyond that he becomes a slave to his property. I have become both slave and thin."

"But I did n't marry a thin man," she said, "and I don't intend to live with one. Don't you think you had better do a little less? Give up one of the gardens?"

"What?" I thundered at her. "Give up a garden?"

"Or hire some one? I was just going to say, 'Or hire some one,' when you bellowed at me. You must n't bellow at me. Remember, I'm your wife."

"Very well," I answered, swallowing my chin. "I will hire some one. This very day I shall."

And that's how the place came to include the Scandinavian.

By Connecticut out of Stockholm, to use the horsey term; by Connecticut forty years out of Stockholm by ten. Not much of a Scandinavian at that, but still speaking of the old country as if it were the Garden of Eden. This I forgive him.

There are three things a man may legitimately romance about — his love affairs previous to marriage, his love affairs since, and the place where he was born.

I met up with him in the midst of a meadow, where he was drawing straight brown lines with a plough across a field of sod. I liked his furrows. I liked his honest eye and I liked the way he talked to his horse. Then and there I dickered with him. He said he was a Seventh-Day Adventist, but worked on Saturdays. He also quoted something out of the Book of Job to back up his claim for more than I had offered. I accepted Job as a superior authority and acquiesced. Then for a while we talked as man to man about cutting lawns, hoeing corn, and cleaning up my establishment. The next day he put in his appearance. He's been there ever since. Under his ministrations order has come out of chaos, two blades have sprung up where only one grew before, and he has solved a problem that, until his arrival, I saw no chance of solving.

IV

BEFORE this current age of modern sanitation an elder generation found it necessary to place serious import upon a certain exterior structural adjunct. I hope to dwell at length and in a scholarly fashion on these some day in Opus No. 50. For

the present it suffices to say that I possessed three
— no less than three — of these structures, scattered at various points of vantage on my seven
acres. And upon them their makers had evidently expended not a little architectural skill.
One was fashioned after the manner of the house
itself — a Greek temple in miniature with a
porch supported by Doric columns. Another
manifested the Georgian influence in its balanced
design and was proudly surmounted by a cupola
in a style to be found to this day in some of the
later houses of Salem. The third leaned toward
Rural Gothic, showing to what depths John
Ruskin dragged otherwise estimable people.

With my own right arm and an axe I demol-
ished the Rural Gothic. The Greek temple was
hauled out of sight. But there still remained the
Georgian structure. Something about its perfect
proportions, about the jaunty set of its half-
moons, stayed my axe. Whenever she asked me
what I intended doing with that thing, I always
changed the subject. Then, as I said, along came
the Scandinavian.

He had not been in my employ a week before I
caught him casting envious glances at that structure. Finally he screwed up his courage and asked
me what I intended doing with it. I was tempted
to tell him that for six months a certain woman of
my acquaintance had been pestering me with that

self-same question. However, I replied, "Nothing."

"Well, if you was n't gona use it," he said, "I can."

"Yes?"

"You see, my wife's sister she's got a daughter what's interested in a young man downtown who has a garage. He needs a tool-house."

Before he could quote Job at me, I answered, "Take it, my man. I consider it an honor to contribute to their hope chest."

I went away for a week and when I returned it was gone.

"I see you've got that moved all right," I remarked. "Did the young man like it?"

"Well, he liked it all right, only I had to take it back. It's down to my place now."

I scented a mystery and looked at him.

"You see, I gave it to him for a tool-house 'longside his garage on Main Street, and he told his neighbors it was a tool-house, but they said they knew a tool-house when they saw one, and it was n't a tool-house. So I had to bring it back."

There was nothing that I could say.

V

THE SPRING AND FALL OF MAN

I

IT is recorded that man was first tempted in a garden, and to this day the temptations of the garden are the most alluring that can be presented to him. Let him once eat of the fruit of the tree that grows in that garden, and his innocence is gone. Thereafter he is eternally conniving, figuring, laboring, indulging himself, slipping more and more under the spell, forgetting more and more his necessary work. He takes up with queer companions. He spends his money like a profligate. He even speaks a strange tongue. Would that a new Milton might arise to write this Spring and Fall of Man!

Lacking a Milton, I take my own pen in hand, I who have passed through all the degrees of temptation down to the depths of an incorrigible gardener. This confession needs must incriminate others. They may forgive me or they may not. These lusty assistants of Satan have no shame; they lure a man on, they whisper things in his ear, they show him the wonders of the world's gardens, they make divine promises.

There was J. Horace McFarland, secretary of

the Rose Society, and otherwise an upright and estimable citizen. Writing me about some business matter, he took the liberty of putting this insidious P.S. to his letter: "Of course, on that country place, you'll grow roses." Up to that moment I had successfully resisted roses. I was saving that virtue to prove that I still had a will of my own. Like my valiant attempt to save gambling.

Through four years of college and many years since I had run the gamut of Decalogue infractions. Some I had only bruised, others I had shattered to bits. But one thing I did not do — I never gambled. I wanted to save that one virtue untouched. I had visions of myself on the last day climbing the steep ascent to the Pearly Gates and being asked by St. Peter what I had left of my primal innocence. Then I would proudly unwrap my handkerchief and show him, sparkling in its folds, the diamond of my solitary unsullied virtue.

The roses were something like that. I had fallen afoul of the astilbe temptation, had become enslaved by collecting clematis, and was a confirmed reprobate on columbines, but I wanted to resist at least one flower temptation. So I wrote to J. Horace in vitriolic terms: "How dare you tempt an innocent, albeit stout, young man? How dare you lay snares in the path of his unsuspecting feet? Garden temptations are about me on all sides, like the fat bulls of Bashan. Valiantly I fight them off. Then you, eminent and respectable, you whisper your insidious, 'Of course, you'll grow roses.' Shame on you!"

After that outburst I thought I had escaped roses. The diamond of my virtue still sparkled like a new engagement ring. Then, one morning, I found her messing around a bed in the newly laid-out formal garden. A large, unopened box stood on the path beside her.

"What are you going to do?" I asked.

"I'm setting out some roses," she replied calmly. My face went white. Tremors shook my frame. "I thought you'd just love to tend them. Think of it — roses, Carissimo!"

Lo, the downfall! I hung my head. I would never be able to climb the steep ascent with confident heart.

II

THE first evidence of the Spring and Fall of man comes about the beginning of February. It is accompanied by seedsmen's catalogues and price lists of pots, labels, watering-cans, and manures. If these can be kept out of his hands, there is a fair chance of his resistance functioning. Once he has opened them, however, there is little hope that it will.

My own collection of catalogues occupied an entire shelf of the library and it is in four tongues, two of which I cannot read. She, who possesses a sense of order, pleads with me to keep them out in the tool-shed, but I am adamant.

I never saw a woman take on so about such harmless things as seed catalogues. Only the other day I overheard her telling Helen Dryden, the artist, who draws the lovely covers for "Vogue," this sort of yarn: "Well, my dear, what can you expect of a man who reads nothing but seed books? When we were first married he used to read me novels and plays and all that sort of thing. Now he never opens a decent book. I find his old catalogues under the bed at night, they litter his desk, he has them in the morning room. I find them tucked behind the clock in the kitchen. How can you expect him to keep his trousers pressed when all he reads is garden catalogues?"

"He's got the catalogue complex," replied Miss Dryden, who lives in Greenwich Village and consequently knows all about psycho-analysis. "It's a psycho-neurosis superinduced by repressed spring weather. Why not ask him why one catalogue is n't enough?"

And she did, sometime later in the day.

"The simplest thing in the world," I answered. "Let me show you." I dumped an armful of

catalogues into her lap and she had to listen.
"Dreer lists only five varieties of aquilegia, but
Sutton shows twelve. I have nineteen growing
here on the place this very minute. Or take
calceolaria — one variety in Dreer, sixteen in
Perry. Think what I would miss! Or clematis —
Bobbink & Atkins list only eleven and Jackman
of Woking has seventy-eight. Or delphiniums —
Henderson lists only four. Imagine it — only
four! Then you turn to Wells of Merstham, and
what do you find? Fifty-five, my girl, fifty-five
varieties of delphinium!"

"Are you going to grow all fifty-five in the
garden?" she asked saucily.

"Well, ah . . ." And I dodged the question
by leading off into a rhapsody on the vast and
varied phlox that Kelway carries.

Although I never acknowledged it to her, the
wiles of the world are tame compared with catalogue temptations. Cards and drink and rois-
tering and vermillion Sundays are as child's play.
There is no devastation comparable with the
complete surrender, the complete corruption of a
man once he has fallen under the spell of gardening catalogues. Like the politicians of Phila-
delphia, he is corrupt and contented.

So exacting a master is it that a man's power
of will is completely subdued. He may honestly
desire to be economical and sensible and fair, but

his good intention will melt in the presence of a catalogue the way ice-cream melts on a hot plate. A man of my acquaintance (he has since gone into the church and repented) once paid forty-eight dollars for a single narcissus bulb. Think of it, forty-eight dollars, the price, in the good old days, of nine hundred and sixty glasses of beer! When it came to choosing between a new dahlia for himself and a new hat for his wife, he got the dahlia.

It was strange, too, about his vocabulary — asparagus was its terminus to the east and in the west he could go no farther than witloof; he knew nothing farther south than abronia, nothing farther north than zinnia. I used to respect his judgment, but my regard began to wane when I saw him lose his balance over the pictures in the catalogues. He actually believed that onions could grow as big as a hat, carrots like thighs, and lupins as tall as steeples. It was fortunate for every one concerned that he caught religion.

The picture-book catalogue has its place because it raises ambition and aspiration in the heart of the amateur gardener, especially the beginner. Like a child he learns the plants from pictures so that, the first year, he won't pull up flowers for weeds. And it is right that aspiration should be stirred up in the heart of man. But the pictured catalogue should not be prized above

others in the library of the incorrigible gardener.
To one long since professed in the vows of gardening, a mere list of names of the varieties suffices; he reads color, form, height, and place in
the garden from the names, the way a trained
musician can take up a score of music and read it
as one does a book.

III

THE second step in the Spring and Fall of man
becomes a veritable field day, a saturnalia, an
orgy, an hilarious "bust." Let the maples begin
to leaf, and he drops his old steady life, his regular
habits, his friends of long standing — and he
disappears. Planting, he'll explain. Nothing of
the sort. He's gone on a seed drunk. That's
what he's done. He's bought far more seeds
than he can ever bring to flower, and he's sticking
them into the ground.

Like a man enslaved to a drug habit, no trouble
is too great or too dangerous for a confirmed gardener to take in order that he may get the seeds of
his dreams. There was my recent visit to Paris,
for example.

Since my French is limited and I never change
my collar until told, she thought it advisable to
accompany me. I might, she said, appear at an
important luncheon in a soiled shirt, which would
ruin my reputation and hurt business. It is

amazing the excuses a woman can think up when she wants to go abroad. Her fears for me were quite unfounded, however. I had been in Paris before and, at that time, like the foolish virgins, had burned my candle at both ends.[9] Parisian nights did n't disturb my dreams any more. Each morning we would walk to the Étoile, salute the Arc de Triomphe, and part, showering blessings on each other for the day. At nightfall, back for dinner and in bed before ten. This going to bed before ten gave us the happy sensation of living in Paris rather than just visiting it.

On the way back home she — she who remembers things an amazing long time — she said, "I can't get over the lamb-like way you behaved in Paris. Bed before ten!"

"Madame, you do not know me," I replied, which was a cryptic saying that I thought best not to elaborate.

A few days before Christmas three large parcels arrived from M. Georges Truffaut's establishment in Versailles.[10] I opened them boldly before her that night. Sixty packets of various aster seeds, for which M. Truffaut is world-famous, fourteen of sweet peas, eight of marigolds, six of baby's-breath, twenty of poppies, an assortment of ageratum, gaillardia, salvia, and other things.

"So that's what you were doing in the day-time," she snorted, "when you said you were at the office! No wonder you wanted to hide your head under the covers before ten!"

I held my peace. When you are caught red-handed, it is always advisable to hold your peace.

"What in thunder do you intend doing with all those seeds?" she demanded.

"Most Wonderful Person," I began, "it is my plan to devote an entire acre to raising annuals. I want to get to know annuals, and there is no better way than by raising them. I shall make that acre blossom like Paradise. I hope also to keep an individual record of each variety and make scientific observations."

"Stuff and nonsense!" she flared back. "You talk like a man in an insane asylum who thinks he is endowed with omnipotence."

"Not quite that bad," I protested.

"No, there are hopes. You may overwork and become satiated and in your satiety revolt against the autocracy of gardening."

"Not a chance, Beloved of my Heart," I replied; "I have the constitution of an ox."

IV

THE third temptation — and by this you may know a man is eternally lost — is to speak a strange language. His native tongue no longer suffices; he needs must converse in Latin and Greek. Does he talk about marigolds? No, he calls them calendulas. The good old name of candytuft, which satisfied generations before him, he dubs iberis. Come on him unawares and you'll hear him murmuring sensuously, the way a small boy rolls a sourball around in his mouth, such strangely succulent words as "salpiglossis," "scabiosa," "sphenogyn." In his exalted moments he will show what a great man he is by pronouncing "sisyrinchium," "hemerocallis," "portenschlogiana," "eschscholtzia," and "mesembryanthemum." He does n't stop to run down the neuter of the second or tick off the feminine of the third declension to find the proper ending; no, he has them exactly. He walks about his garden chatting a Latin as far above reproach as Cæsar's wife.

I first learned to speak garden Latin from my father (blessed be his name!). He said that I need never be ashamed of it, that it would make me brother to the little Jap sitting beside his stone garden lantern in Yamagani, to the devout Moslem in his Omar Khayyám garden, to some exquisite daughter of France bending over 'her Legion of Honor marigolds, to the strictly proper person in Lenox, Massachusetts, surveying her formal estate. To all of us *rosa* must always be the rose. And so it has come about; wars may warp the temper of people, they may change the names of their cities and their boulevards, Bolshevism may rise and kings depart, still the humble tradescantia Virginiana var. coccinea remains the humble tradescantia Virginiana var. coccinea — that gentle little flower in the cranny of the wall, the red spiderwort.

When the gardener has reached the Latin stage, he is beyond recall. His family and friends may as well give him up. He no longer cares for fine clothes or whist or social progress or making lots of money or becoming a power in the land, to which normal people are said to devote themselves. From that time on he'll earn his bread by the sweat of his brow and be proud of it. He'll take his interest in flowers and let the credit go. He'll count his capital in potatoes. He'll rejoice in rotted manures and blabber about mulch. His dream will be delphiniums towering behind madonna lilies and three heights of snapdragons flirting in the sun.

He makes a sorry figure, this fallen man. His hands are always dusty and his trousers bagged at the knees. He goes about with silent mien and communicates in grunts. He flies into a passion should any innocent neighbor have peas before he has them. He struts like a peacock when he plucks the first corn in his town. He writes letters to men and women in distant parts, long communications about geums and how to treat them, and what to do for rose aphids. Mad, utterly mad!

V

THIS is a very serious condition, this Spring and Fall of man. It is an annual, insidious devastation of the manhood and womanhood of America. How can it be stopped? How can the temptation be removed?

You Comstocks of the world, you Andersons and Crafts and would-be Savonarolas, I ask you, what are you going to do about it? I defy you, by the bones of all the martyrs, I defy you to stop us in our perilous course! If you amend the Constitution forbidding the sale of seed, we gardeners will grow them at home! If you fling us into jail, we'll raise flowers in the cracks of our prison walks!

Harken, brethren of the blue nose and white tie! There is no solution for this terrible indulgence. You have to bow before the reality of the fact. We gardeners are tempted more than we are able, and we're damned proud of it. The only way to get rid of this temptation is to yield to it, you abominable reformers. The only way for you to handle us floral drunkards is to become flower-sots yourselves.

Thank Heaven, there's no amending us out of that Eden once we've passed inside its gate.

"He who has a garden, still his Eden keeps."

VI
ON A WINTER OF DISCONTENT

I

LIFE in the original Eden, though, must have been rather dull. No ministers prating about the shortness of skirts, no college professors showing their senility by calling silk stockings an evil, no Blue Sundays, no Prohibition, no Anti-Cigarette Campaign. No Spring. No Summer. No Autumn. What did Adam and Eve do for thrills? It is terrible to contemplate, this not having the capacity or the opportunity for a thrill.

And yet even I had gotten to the pass where nothing thrilled me. The anticipation of Christmas morning left me cold. I accepted my pay envelope of Friday nights without a tremor. I could see a pretty face in a crowd and continue on just as if I had n't had that glimpse of ultimate beauty.[11] It appeared as though — so my friends said — I was headed for the oblivion of a fatty and comfortable middle age. When a man gets in that condition something has to happen to him; he needs an emotional jolt. I had it — Spring.

In that first autumn our intentions were enormous, our dreams amazingly vast. If my friend

John Scheepers had sold me all the bulbs and roots I had intended planting, he could have retired for life. Night after late summer night we pored over the catalogues. We grew groggy, like fighters in the final round. Now an upper cut of beauty from an "Albert Crousse" peony sent us staggering. Now we swayed with a nasty knuckle-blow from a "Mme. Chereau" iris. Then came a stunner straight in the eye from a meadowful of "Silver Phœnix" narcissus. We yielded and took the count when hyacinth "King of Blues" showered blows upon us.

The insidious part about yielding to these catalogue temptations lies in the fact that the pleasure flowers afford is the most innocent pleasure in the world and a fellow feels so all-powerful virtuous about it. You can think up so many perfectly legitimate excuses for spending money on flowers.

An honored parent told us precisely what sort of fools we were for putting all that money under the ground, and he almost had us repenting. The next spring, when he saw that border riotous with "Mme. Schroeder" peonies, he succumbed and took it all back.

Solomon was wrong. Don't heap coals of fire upon the head of your enemy; shower him with flame-colored Darwins, preferably "Princess Juliana" or "Clara Butt." If your enemy disagrees

with you, let the sun go down if it pleases, but
after it does, collect her an armful of cactus
dahlias. Before I was married, I used to say
things with books, luncheons, theater tickets, and
Sherry's candy, but she — she whose eyes
brightened even at the violent beds of ageratum
and salvia in the gardens of the Tuileries — she
is now quite overcome when I lay in her lap the
first mauve little primula.

Eve made a great mistake: she said it with an
apple. Had she said it with flowers, the course of
the world might have been altered.

We wrote our intentions all over the place that
autumn. In addition to naturalizing a multitude
of narcissus and crocus, in one long border we put
a backbone of peonies and iris with shoals of
tulips here and there to give the early garden its
touches of rich color. The former owner planted
funkias along the kitchen wing, and into these we
introduced the soft salmon rose of "Clara Butt"
and the vermillion scarlet of "Glow." It was
frankly an experiment, along the same lines of
economical gardening that made Miss Jekyll (or
was it Mrs. Francis King?) suggest planting tulips in the fern bed. At points along the herbaceous border there went in clumps of "Europe,"
a glowing salmon scarlet; "White Queen," colored
like its name; "La Tonnaye," a blush-shaded rose;
and some "Mrs. Farcombe Sanders," that scarlet

with a clear white base. "William Pitt" went
under the shadow of a fir tree, hard by a lilac
bush, a planting that, when I wrote a well-known
gardening authority about it, elicited polite scorn.

Apropos of this I must state my heterodoxy.
Unless a flower combination is utterly bad, unless
the colors clang and clash together like old tin pots
in a gunny sack, I see no reason why the gardener
should n't combine any colors that please him or
her, gardening authorities to the contrary. She
must not take her garden gods from a printed
book.

Of the making of garden books there is no end,
and the reading of too many of them is a vain
pursuit that leads to confusion. I would withhold
a lot of them from the beginner, just as I would
advise college students to refrain from reading
Nietzsche till after they are thirty. Both bring
bewilderment. In fact, Nature herself is a book
that should not be read at too-extended sittings.

The beginning gardener should first plant in the
fashion that pleases her; she will attain her garden
wisdom gradually, change the planting, and finally arrive at the color and leafage combinations
that delight her most. The one thing for her to
remember is that there is n't any rule about it.
Moses did n't come down from his Mount of
Vision with an edict on flowers.

II

ALONG about the middle of December we were
struck by a devastating thought. We have these
devastating thoughts right along, as you will
observe. It was to this effect: had we planted all
our bulbs and perennials in the right way? You
know the terror in the heart of the young mother
(unfortunately, I never can) when she realizes
that she has fed the baby milk boiled longer than
the directions require? Possibly the poor little
thing will die of spasms that very night! That's
how I felt when, this mid-December noon, while
we were having luncheon at Henri's, she asked me,
"Forgive my mentioning it, but did you put some
well-rotted manure under those delphiniums?"

"No," I answered, looking up from my *petite
marmite*, "nor did I plant all the tulips in sand
nor give all the narcissus a handful of bone meal."

"We probably shan't have a single blossom!"
she sighed.

I assured her that we doubtless would, but if
we did n't I'd get some more next year. Vain
consolation! My neglect almost ruined that
lunch.

In naturalizing these narcissus we followed the
time-honored custom of punching holes. What
with her punching the holes and my setting the
bulbs, we put in a pretty busy day. Then, when

we had finished and returned to the city, I met up with Frank Galsworthy. Now, Frank is as good a gardener as John is a novelist. An artist of flowers by choice, a grower of flowers by sheer love of 'em, and, if I might mention a gentlemanly trait of the old school, a delectable taker of snuff.

Said Frank, offering me his snuff-box, "How did you plant those narcissus?"

"Punch and plant," I replied, accepting the hospitality.

"Wrong! Wrong, my boy, utterly wrong. At my place at Chertsey, I grow narcissus by the thousands, seas of them, lovely beyond compare, and this is how it is done. You skin back the turf of your meadow or orchard just as if you were taking it up for sodding. Spade in some bone meal. Place in the bulbs. Roll back the turf and tramp it down. Very simple."

Some day we shall try that.

The conversation led me to think of what I am pleased to call sub-surface gardening. I don't see why an all-wise Providence or the Paleolithic man did n't arrange for this layer of bone meal or well-rotted manure six to eighteen inches below the surface of garden soils. It would have saved us all an immense amount of trouble. I neglect it right along, and yet I know, as well as I know that I'm thwacking this Corona, that the secret of good gardening lies in the sub-surface prepara-

tion. A narcissus bulb may live off itself, as a
Sinn Feiner lives off himself during a hunger
strike, and still produce wonderful flowers. Thousands of the polyanthus type do every winter,
planted in bowls of pebbles and water. But when
they have given themselves to this exhausting
extent, they want to rest and eat. The bulb in
the bowl has no wherewithal to eat, as does the
bulb in the soil, and consequently is done,
through, annihilated. That little pinch of bone
meal scattered in the bottom of the hole before
naturalizing a bulb is the food always ready in
the larder. That layer of well-rotted manure is
the three-meals-a-day of hundreds of plants.

III

It was along in March that I discovered the road.
How I ever had missed it, I don't know. It came
about this way:

The winter of my discontent was getting a little
too heavy to bear. I simply had to see that garden, that house. We were slated to go to luncheon and a tea-party, but I would have nothing of
them. "Make the best excuses you can," I said,
departing, "but I must consult with my Bellis
Perennis." An hour later I was knee-deep in snow.

There had been a prodigious snow-fall the past
week and no teams had broken our uphill road.
By going across lots, above stone walls, and past

the roofs of corn cribs I finally managed the top
of our hill. A primeval stillness lay about on all
sides. It was still the way the world will be still
when this old globe finally goes cold. I scrabbled
in the snow, down through a heavy mulch of
leaves, and finally uncovered a plant or two of
English daisy, fresh and green. Then I covered it
up carefully and kicked back the snow. I could
now go back to New York quite satisfied. The
world could wag on!

And I was about to turn back across the field
trainward when a sudden impulse made me beat
a path through the virgin snow up to the kitchen
garden, the highest point on our hill. Ah, such a
lovely sight! The valley houses looked so close
that I could have pitched stones into their chim-
neys. The big country house on the ridge beyond
us stood out naked and near. My orchard was
within an arm's reach, it seemed; the white
swathe where the road lay, at my very feet. I
could have picked it up, as one picks up a bit of
ribbon thrown carelessly on the floor. Then I
turned to see where that ribbon road went — and
lo, it went out of sight! It turned, it ducked, it
twisted around a corner.

I had been on that road every day for months
and it never had occurred to me that something
might lie beyond my house. Here I stood on the
verge of romance, and knew it not. Beyond lay

the ridge of cedars and bare rock that we call Doglands, and behind Doglands the road had ducked. I broke down through the steep bank, plunged into the hip-deep snow at the bottom, and followed that road to its bend. For a few hundred yards it lay before me straight and even. I could mark it by the hollow and the fringe of bush-tops peeping out of the snow on either side. Then it ducked around another corner and was again lost to sight. A most exasperating road!

On the ridge beyond stood a cozy-looking farmhouse with its barns and outbuildings clustered about it like a mother hen with chicks. And behind that a wood, dark and somber.

"Go on!" something shouted at me. "Go on! Follow it!" But the snow was too deep. It was all I could do to gain my tracks again and head downhill.

I had seen a new world, though, and I knew the road to it now. . . . And to this day, when I want to get away from bothersome things, I take the turn of that road and lose myself in the world of romance. Every new road we walk upon is a highway to a new world.

IV

THEN, as I said, came Spring.

It is among the peculiarities of poets that in their ecstasies on Spring they almost invariably picture it as a sort of glorified fairy in diaphanous wraps — "a glimmering girl with apple blossoms in her hair" — who comes tiptoeing down the land to touch the flowers and trees and bushes and make them leap into blossom.

Very pretty!

For the life of me I simply can't visualize Spring as a perfect thirty-six in Moon Glow silk tripping up and down my seven acres more or less. If I must compare it to a woman, let her be oldish and stout and far from innocent.

To me Spring is a movement, a mighty surging upward. It is n't coaxed from above, but moved from below. The growing things break upward through the crust of chill earth the way a man gets out of bed on a zero morning — gradually, reluctantly, cover by cover, a toe at a time; not because some one has waked him, but because he has accumulated the necessary refreshment of sleep and is ready to go forth and do the day's work.

That day's work may not be anything very strenuous, and yet it has a purpose. The earliest flowers in the garden are usually small flowers — as if Nature herself were putting out a toe at a time — snowdrops, crocus, and scillas. If these can stand it, then she comes out flat-footed on the cold floor of the earth with hyacinths, narcissus, tulips, and iris pumila. Once up, she shivers into a kimono of leafing trees, washes her face with April rains, does up her hair into delightful flowering shrubs, and sallies forth — the vain old thing! — in a gorgeous creation of peonies and German iris and lush green grass.

Thus the old jade came to us that first year — splendidly arrayed, pompous, odorous with violets and the sweet smell of spring bonfires.

VII

FROM THE WELL-HEAD TO THE DRY WALL

I

HAVING dismissed the carpenter, we thought we were through with him. As we watched him stride down the path with our final cheque clutched in his hand it seemed as if we could close that chapter. From somewhere the money had come. But the miracle would never happen again. You must n't count on miracles. You may believe in them; that is all right. But never figure, when you see a carpenter's bill for $1258 coming toward you, that a miracle will put that $1258 in your pocket. Feeling this way about it, we thought it best not to tempt Providence again. Providence had acted like a lamb about the first bill. No, it was wiser never to see that carpenter again.

This was a vain resolution, for we needed a pergola, a number of trellises, and, above all, a well-head.

Choosing the design for a well-head is even more difficult than picking out a wedding present. Once wedding presents became such a problem that I finally was obliged to give the same present to all brides — a coffee percolator. Young or old, pretty or plain, rich or poor, each received a percolator. Then my good intentions were badly smashed in a matrimonial jam; I gave a percolator twice to the same bride within the space of three years. Husband No. 1 went the way of Reno. When she saw the second percolator among the second marriage presents, she confided to me that the first was n't anywhere near worn out yet. Since then I have given linen, of which I am led to believe, no woman can ever have too much.

The selection of the design for that well-head consisted mainly in a cross-fire of chatter and back-chat.

"Well-head?" I blustered. "What sort of well-head?"

"There are dozens of kinds," she protested.

"Name them, Madame," I said.

"We might pick up the capital of some old Roman column," she answered calmly, "and have it hollowed out."

"Very quaint!" I replied.

"Or we might buy one of these perfectly dear old English lead baths and use that," she rambled on.

"Perfectly dear is right," I commented. "Perfectly out of the question would be more like it."

"Or we could have it made of brick or wood or rustic timber," she concluded.

"Your feet are almost touching the earth," was my reply.

"Personally I abhor rustic work," she said emphatically. "It always reminds me of a man who needs a shave."

"Why not plain boards?" I gave as my contribution.

"Every one has them."

"A well-sweep, then," I suggested.

"Too arty," came her comment.

I held my peace, knowing that sooner or later she would — as she usually does — arrive at some perfectly delightful scheme.

"I'll tell you what!" She snapped her fingers. "The well-curb itself shall be built of brick and will be painted white like the foundations of the house. The canopy over it shall be of wood, painted like the roof."

"May I paint the ceiling of that canopy blue?" I asked — "like the ceiling of the terrace roof?"

"It is possible that you may be permitted," she answered regally.

And thus the well-head was built — square at the bottom, of brick, with a broad flat lip to give the curb finish. This has been painted white with my own hand. The elements will wash off some of that paint, thus ageing the brick, as we desire. The supports are square timbers, white as the bark of a young birch. And the ceiling of the roof, where the wheel for the bucket rope is concealed. has been painted a heavenly blue. Some day I shall spatter it with gold stars and place there the sign of Sagittarius.

This passion for gold stars and the signs of the zodiac has doubtless been superinduced by walking twice a day under the ceiling of the Grand Central Station. I also have a feeling that we should have about us in our homes occasional reminders of those things which to men at one time were sacred, on which they pinned their faith and by which they guided their lives. A dryad peeping out of a shrubbery hedge can remind us that the old gods may not all be dead. The symbol of St. Agnes that hangs on the guest-room door — that delectable Yellow Room — reminds us of a beautiful maiden done to death by the Romans, who in that hour is reputed to have exclaimed—

> If I love Him I shall be chaste,
> If I touch Him I shall be clean,
> If I embrace Him, I shall be virgin indeed! [13]

And these signs of the zodiac that I hope to paint about the place will say, as I look up at them: "Don't be so sure, my boy! The Protestant Episcopal Church may not control the exclusive rights to the future. These old Greeks and Chaldeans, who charted the course of man's destiny according to Capricornus and Aries and Gemini, may still have the last laugh!"

That is why, when next the house is painted, the porches fore and aft will have blue ceilings on which will be laid in fine gold a Milky Way of stars and the twelve signs of the little animals that once meant a great deal to men.

II

SPEAKING of the stars reminds me of something I thought out one hot afternoon when I was hoeing cabbages. It was a series of disconnected thoughts evolved between hacks at the earth. The conclusions may not be tenable, but, as I later put down the thoughts, they pleased me. They were to this effect.

That a garden is not merely a place to look at; it is a place to look from. And the way to look from a garden is to look up. More, a garden is not alone a place to work in; it is a place to work from. And the way to work from a garden is to work upward.

These are hard sayings, as the Bible puts it, so I shall try to explain them.

Three things bring us to the earth and three things hold us to it. The soil is very old. Its traditions are unchanging. And its fruits are for the benefit of all men

The soil from which he sprang — that is the

soil the gardener touches. The soil which he can make to bear abundantly — that is the soil whose traditions stabilize the gardener's life. The soil to which he shall eventually return — that is the soil to breed his noblest dreams.

Because he is part of it, once he has known the touch of the soil. It is to him as something of his own flesh, an *alter ego*, an abiding companion, trustworthy if trusted, abundant if disciplined. This fundamental dependability holds a man to the soil once he has known the touch of it. And touching it has a very salutary effect: it cleanses him of popinjay notions, it rids him of futile materialism. It acts as a spiritual cathartic.

It is ludicrous to be cynical in the presence of a lusty oak breaking into leaf. It is impossible to be decadent with loam upon your hands. And you can't be fashionable or superbly intellectual as you guide the plough. These things simply won't work. They don't belong. The realm of Nature is a different world, where such affairs are of no consequence. Therefore, if you would understand the soil, you must learn its tongue; and before you can learn it, you are obliged to clear away your false notions, to forget the jargon of cities and books and ballrooms.

The gardener may oftentimes be a fool, but he will be a divine fool. "Eyes and ears," said Heraclitus, "are bad witnesses to those who have

barbarian souls." And an appalling number of
people have barbarian souls. The city breeds
them by countless thousands. They judge by eyes
and ears, and by them alone. The gardener
judges otherwise. His soul is the reflection of
divine paradoxes — like a man dying that he may
live, or selling the world that he may gain his
soul. The gardener slashes the soil that he may,
in turn, heal the wound with flowers — or cabbages!

It is said of mystics (I have read it somewhere)
that they all speak the same language because
they all come from the same country. Gardeners
all speak the same tongue because they all touch
the same soil. They hear flowers that sound and
see notes that shine. Enraptured, they listen to
the great fugue of succeeding blossoms. Their
harvest of joy is as obvious and intangible as the
blue sky above. Let a man feel the magic of the
soil, and lo, his eyes are opened! How was it
William Blake argued this point? — "The tree
which moves some to tears of joy," he said, "is,
in the eyes of others, only a green thing that
stands in the way."

Now, if you have noticed it, you will discover
that these men who live daily with Nature, and
whose hands are bronzed with her loam, have a
quaint way of speaking. They use fantastically
simple images and are gifted with a native brand

of poetry that sounds not unlike some passages of the Bible read. There is a rhythm to their tongue that other men simply can't acquire.

Nature has a rhythm all her own, a rhythm so entirely different from the concatenation of cities, that a man has to be purged of his city ways before he can understand it. He has to acknowledge that there is a vast cosmos outside the little circle in which he moves and has his being. Once he acknowledges this, he becomes a neophyte in that vaster world, he is permitted a glimpse into that cosmos and hears the echo of its songs. It is this unearthly singing that makes the speech of farmers sound so strange.

In the eternal dominion of Nature there is a great movement constantly circling upward, as the lark circles upward, and those who come close to her are swept along with it. A man soon learns this when he starts working in a garden. He can't resist its cleansing. He can't resist the tug of its other-worldly urging or the uprush of its hidden energy from the deep silences of the earth. Consequently, the longer he works in that garden, the more he is compelled to work the way Nature works — upward

III

I MIGHT have continued these thoughts (perhaps I shall in a later chapter) had not the Scandinavian broken in upon them. He approached respectfully and reported that it was done, "it" being a newly relaid stretch of wall in which I hope to do some dry wall gardening. To my amazement, he had done it just as I had told him.

The stones of a wall that is to be planted — and this holds true of all rock gardening — must be laid on the slant so that pockets of earth will be formed into which the roots can run downward and in which the moisture can be conserved. Alpine plants do not demand much soil, but they do demand a toe-hold and good drainage at the roots. If you are so fortunate as to have a wall of limestone, the alpinii will be quite in their native habitat; where sandstone or other kinds of rocks are used, it is advisable to scatter in the soil some rough pieces of mortar to give it sweetness.

This stretch of dry wall runs along the road — New England boulders and split rock with a flat ledge along the top. One of these days when I have time and the season is right, it will be planted to purple rock cress, creeping chalk plant, rock speedwell, white and pink stonecrop, tufted harebell, alpine asters, pink saxifrage and golden asters, with phlox subulata and woolly thyme on the top of the wall.

Rock gardening, which has become such a finished art in England, is still in its infancy with

us; not that there are n't many wonderful rock
gardens in America, but because there is n't the
general enthusiasm for them as on the other side.

The joy of the rock garden is the joy of the
intime and *petite*. Unless it is built on a large
scale, and arabis and creeping phlox are depended
.upon for big, bold "swatches" of color and grasses
for higher accent points, it can never be precisely a showy garden in the way that a perennial
border is showy. On the other hand, it is not a
toy affair; rather, rock gardening is to floriculture
what miniatures, engraved gems, coins, and'Chinese snuff-bottles are to the collector.

IV

AND that brings up a problem which sooner or
later confronts every lover of flowers; namely, to
what extent should his garden be a collection? If
the garden is planted for certain effects of color
and foliage, then a few varieties should be used
and those in masses. The other day I saw an
English shrubbery planting that called for fifty-
nine varieties of shrubs in a smallish corner plan.
It reminded me of the sort of thing the local
nurseryman will do if you don't watch him.
Everything but the kitchen stove. Now a rock
garden may be a collection of alpine plants, but
the shrubbery planting and herbaceous border
cannot be merely collections unless one wants

them to look like Sam Hill. On the other hand, it may be well for the beginning gardener to try a little of everything. If he watches each plant, studies its requirements, and notes its general effect, he will have a good working basis on which to develop his garden as the years go on.

Personally I have a great weakness for this sort of collecting. I enjoy gambling in as much of a genus as I can argue my accusing conscience and limited purse into accepting. There is space enough back of the kitchen garden to put such things in row on row, like a nursery. I have done that to a range of astilbe and have ever since blessed the name of George Arend[13] for his great work in this flower. A range of clematis has been planted at odd and inoffensive corners of the place, which makes me think respectfully of Jackman[14] of Woking every time I see them. And as for annuals — but my respect for annuals deserves a chapter all to itself.

VIII

THE KITCHEN THAT WAS N'T GREEK

I

At this point I was going to begin an elaborate defense of annuals, when she — she who invariably snores when I read her what I have written — she impolitely peeked over my shoulder.

"Ump!" she snorted. "I thought you were writing a book about our place in the country. You've devoted fifty pages to the garden and three to the decorations of the house. The house is far more important than the garden."

Thus far in writing this book I had followed the well-known principle of going ahead without permission — on the theory of Roosevelt's taking the Panama Canal site and asking confirmation for it afterward. Or like the old lady who told a friend: "My dear, I never ask permission to do anything. Never! If I did, I'd get scolded before I did it and scolded afterward. If you go ahead without asking permission, you get scolded only once. It is a great saving on the nerves." As this was only the first scolding, I really did n't mind.

As I have explained before, apropos of putting the signs of the zodiac on the ceilings of the porches, I thought there ought to be something

Greek about the place. But I bumped my head against modern realities when I offered suggestions for fixing over the kitchen in the manner of Hellas. It can't be done. You simply can't make walls of Troy fit in with blue-flame stoves and patent garbage buckets. Resignedly I laid aside my own fair plans, put my Liddell & Scott lexicon on the topmost shelf, and went out to contemplate the sunset.

And yet that kitchen is an achievement. The walls are the color of tub butter — not this anæmic sort of butter you buy ready wrapped in quarter-pound packages, but the full, rich yellow of butter *en masse*. Four windows light it, facing east and south, and a skylight that, from the outside, looks like the hatch of a ship. I never before saw a kitchen with a skylight that looked like the hatch of a ship; perhaps you have n't either. At the windows hang curtains of dotted Swiss edged with blue rickrack which, of course, contrasts happily with the butter-yellow walls. Between the two front windows stands a cottage table painted yellow and blue, with a high-back yellow-and-blue chair on each side of it. Above, on the wall, hangs a blue-and-yellow Italian majolica plate. That Italian plate is the nearest this kitchen ever got to Greece.

Some day, when I receive that heritage from a certain relative who has been dying and going to leave me it ever since I was a small boy, some day, when Charon rows back that ship loaded to the gunwales with gold, I hope to hang on the kitchen walls fine French prints of ancient kitchens and the culinary arts. I may also form a kitchen library of old kitchen books and works on gastronomy — Audat's "La Cuisinière de la Campagne et de la Ville"; the fifty-nine numbers of "Gastronomie, Revue de l'Art Culinaire Ancien et Modern," Fulbert-Dumonteil's "L'Art de Bien Manger," together with such modern works in England as "The White House Cook Book," "Mrs. Rorer," "The One Hundred and Sixty-six Menus of the Baron Brisse," Fannie Farmer's "Boston Cooking-School Cook Book," and, as a final touch, Ellwanger on "The Pleasures of the Table." Peeping in these might induce our blessed Mélaine to change her menus a little from the day-in and day-out *poulet avec pomme frite* and *jambon avec pinard*.

The real achievement in the kitchen was the built-in cupboard, which fills two sides of one corner. It has all manner of cubby-holes and sliding shelves and trick closets for trick electrical equipment and thin ones for trays and fat ones for flower bowls. The carpenter almost gave us notice when he worked on it a day. It really is worth-while, though, this cupboard, and on these broad shelves are marshaled a diverse array of

plates and tureens and cups and what-not that
delight the heart of woman.

II

MY neighbor, the oldest inhabitant, has confided
to me that the man who put on that kitchen wing
to my Greek temple was lazy; he was too lazy
to dig out a few more spades of earth and put the
floor on the level of the adjoining hall. That sort
of laziness should be rewarded. I hope he is now
resting in peace and has chocolate souflée to eat
every day, and cherubim to play him Tschai-
kovsky's "Andante Cantabile" whenever he
wants to hear it. That step down from the kitchen
to the floor of the lower hall is one of the pleas-
antest details of the house.

Thus, you step out of a butter-yellow and del-
phinium-blue kitchen to a hallway with a color
scheme of butter-yellow and zinnia-red, the red
predominating. I like that hall paper; to quote
Eugene Field, I like any color so long as it is red.
Besides, who but she would think to put red on
a little dark hall? You come from the front path
where the sun blinds you into this chromatic
jolt. It hits you in the eye. Hoffman of Vienna
made the original design, a rollicking cross-patch
full of funny yellow whirligigs. When I asked
her why she chose it, she replied, cryptically,
"Some things I do because they are right, others
because I like to."

Hard by the front door in this hall is the make-up shelf — a shelf which holds a long, narrow, painted old Spanish box with pieces of mirror inside its lid. Above it hangs a mirror in a painted frame to match. The box contains such delightful artificialities as rouge, powder, lip-sticks, eye-brow pencils, powder puffs, patches, and a scent atomizer. You stop on the way to dinner to give a last dab to your nose or straighten an eyebrow or affix a patch.

I do not hold with those puny Savonarolas who rush their sermons into every Monday paper, proclaiming these things to be wrong. It does not shock me to learn that in the year of grace 1920 no less than eighty million dollars was spent in the United States on face-powder alone. I do not have a qualm talking to a girl with rouge upon her cheeks, or soot on her eyebrows. None of these things fool me. No man is fooled by such things, as H. L. Mencken has learnedly observed in one of his books, nor is he dragged down to Hell by them. That make-up shelf is our mutual protest — hers and mine — against this most absurd of absurd preachments.

III

AND having powdered your nose, you step across the hall into the dining-room. Rather, you walk through the dining-room onto the terrace, for, save in the most extreme and inclement weather, our dining is done out of doors.

Personally I think a dining-room is the most overrated part of a house and I would dispense with it altogether. Is it necessary to have a special chapel devoted to the worship of the Goddess Gasteria? Here is a room that works only about two hours a day; the rest of the time it is just occupying space, like an empty church. It is a relief to find, in some of the modern plans for small houses, no provision for a dining-room. This gives a large living-room, at one end of which the dining-table can be placed. When company comes, it is a simple matter to screen this end off or pull out doors concealed in the wall. This screen should be provided, not because guests object to seeing a table being set, but because it gives them the pleasure of surprise — that sudden turning a corner and coming upon a table with fine napery and candles alight and the crystal glistening. Half the fun of dining out is this surprise — the other half is the change in diet.

So this is a dining-room that isn't a dining-room. The equipment is here — a big fireplace with a monolithic hearth and a cavernous opening, a low wainscot with rough plaster above, and a long refectory sort of table with Italian chairs standing about like good children. Here also are curtains of yellow casement cloth with a woolly fringe of blue, a scheme that has a method. For in this dining-room that is n't a dining-room are hung her lights.

I have no explanation for why people collect the things they do. Why should an otherwise sane and virile man collect bandboxes. Why should a publisher collect Chinese snuff-bottles? Why should a theatrical producer spend his every odd moment and every last thousand dollars buying up old Mandarin coats? Why did she hit on lights? Why did n't it happen to be laces or French bibelots or patch-boxes or miniatures? Solomon may be puzzled by the ways of a man with a maid and a snake on a rock, but I'm more puzzled by collectors. It is one of those things in life that you simply have to accept — and be the richer for accepting. She's never too tired to talk about her lights or how she got them and how they were used. It is a great gift, the collector's.

Here's a five-pointed drip lamp of hammered brass from Provence; yonder an old-fashioned Southern stairway candle-lamp with an adjustable glass shield, beside it a ship's Gimbel light, that swings with the roll and tosses with the toss. Close by the fire stands a Breton hearth-light of wrought iron with a rosin dip, the sort that is lighted of fête days. Above it is suspended a Moorish lantern, a queer Turkish hanging lamp with a long glass font, a hook candlestick from the Dolomites, and a Betty lamp of bronze. Along the mantel shelf range an assortment of Hanukah lights, tin Colonial sconces, Jewish seven-branch candlesticks, a Roman lamp of brass, and a Spanish church light. A number of flat Roman clay lamps stand on a little side table and in the corner hangs a harem light that must have a history. From the West Indies come those strange lamps made of medicine bottles and odd bits of tin; from Japan an assortment of candlesticks. Outside the terrace is lighted at night by an old Seville church lamp that used to burn before the Presence. It casts its strange glow up on the blue ceiling, the ceiling as blue as the Virgin's robe.

Behind the dining-room is the cellar. In there are rats.

IV

OR, to be more precise, in there *were* rats.

But for those rats we should have had no terror, no destruction, no fiery indignation, no breathless fight, no going to early church of a certain Sunday morning.

The house had been unoccupied for a fortnight and I came back to it jovially. Home again! But my joy snapped.

There are two terrors that have no equal —

to come home and find that your house has been
ransacked by burglars and to come home and
find that your house has been invaded by rats.
A visitation of burglars (we had three in the space
of five short months) is a terrific emotional strain
because it so utterly makes you lose your faith
in humanity; you go about for days hopelessly
asking yourself, "Why? But why must men do
such things?" Rats are another kind of emotional strain, the strain of fierce and destructive
wrath, murderous, torturous, hideous, blasphe-
mous wrath. You may argue, plead, dicker and
bargain with a burglar, but there is no bar-
gaining with a rat. You can't appeal to his finer
sensibilities, to the fact that he, too, had a mother;
when you see a rat, you kill it.

Finding that a rat had devoured all of the blankets on my cot in Orphant Annie's room and had
devastated the bed in the Blue Room, I strode
around like a madman. I put it up to the barn
door; I told the study walls all about it; I asked
God politely but firmly why rats were ever permitted to exist. The crow that pulls up my corn
I can understand. The robin that eats all my
cherries I sympathize with. I know the why and
wherefore of bees, snakes, rabbits, and hawks.
But I simply can't get the rat through my head.
Having thus apostrophised the empyrean, I
went downtown and bought traps and poison.

Then we held a council of war, down in the lower hall at the foot of the stairs, with the red paper on all sides making us see redder. She in her best French and I in my worst, which is my best, Mélaine and I debated as to where these traps should be placed to the best advantage. She had a theory on the *salle de bain*, I held out for the morning room. We were about to compromise on my study when something black loped up the stairs before our very eyes. Its tail wriggled playfully as it disappeared through the door. The damned rat!

We pursued, armed with poker and fire-tongs, hissing curses that would have made Jack the Ripper pale with envy. Upstairs and down, beneath beds and in cupboards, behind books and under chairs. For hours we searched for that rat, carefully closing each door and avenue of escape behind us. We scoured every corner of the Blue Room, the Yellow Room, and her Apricot Room. We took Orphant Annie's room to pieces. My study went the way of Belgium and the bathroom the way of Serbia. We searched with torch and candle and lamp. We scoured the house from four in the afternoon till ten at night. Only fatigue made us give it up.

At dawn the next day I awoke suddenly. Something was gnawing. I listened. Yes, the damned rat! I could hear him squeak and scamper. It

came from the Blue Room — and the Blue Room
door was closed. Mr. Rat was there, and there
he would stay until I could slay him. Mélaine
was roused for the battle. She averred, seizing
the poker, that she had n't slept a wink all night
for thinking of rats. But there was no time for
sympathy. I ran up to the barn and brought a
spade and a fork. Then we slipped in.

He had had a fine night of it. The carpet and
doorsill were gnawed. The window frames were
gnawed. He had almost completed a hole in the
cupboard floor. Somewhere in that room was a
rat who was destined to die young; one of those
infant prodigies who, as the Bible puts it, accomplished a great deal in a short time.

Cautiously we lifted the mattress. No rat.
The springs. No rat. The cupboard was emptied.
No rat. We contemplated the room for a minute,
helplessly — gazed upon the pretty painted bed
and the bureau with the blue morning-glories
growing up its front. No sign of a rat and no
sound. Then we pulled open the top bureau
drawer. Still no rat. The second. Never a sign
of him. Where in blazes could he be? The third—
ah! — Bang! Clash! Bing! Curse! We dashed
after him from corner to corner. We whacked
and punched and thrust. We tried Joffre's
maneuver on the Marne and Pershing's at
Château-Thierry. Finally, with a mighty oath,

such as the French hurled at Waterloo, Mélaine sent the fork at him. He did not move. We carried him out triumphantly on the spade.

"Well, it's only seven o'clock," I remarked when I had got my breath.

"Is monsieur ready for his breakfast?" she asked, being the almost-perfect servant.

"No, it's a little too early," I answered. "But you'd be just in time for church."

So the old jitney was wound up, and through the cool October morning we rode off across the hills.

It was a strange preparation for Mass:

IX

FEEDING AMONG THE LILIES

I

THERE is much to be said for the good, old-fash-ioned porch, the sort with turkey-red chairs where one sat through a lazy afternoon, feet on the railing, hat over his eyes, and bliss in his heart. Such porches were a distinctive mark of Americanism, and it is to President Harding's credit that he chose the porch as his rostrum. But if we don't keep an eye on them, these architect fellows will rob us of our porches. They are flooding the countryside with English cottages, Italian villas, and French châteaux, on none of which the porch can be successfully grafted. Now and then they concede us a glass-enclosed sun-room or a paved terrace, but the old-fashioned porch is anathema to them.

This is a great pity, for the porch serves a definite purpose; it is to the house what white flowers are to a border — it marks a transition. We should n't have to go abruptly from a garden into a house or *vice versa*. The progress should be gradual — from the sun-flooded lawn to the half-shade of the porch, thence on to the full, cool darkness of the house itself.

I grant you, there is something picturesque about a paved terrace with a yellow-and-red awning stretched across it; there is a romantic quality about an Italian courtyard with shades of deep red Venetian sail cloth, but neither of these has the permanent character that a porch gives.

Being by way of Boston out of Italy she — she, who has traveled much — she stood out for the terrace, and, to back up her contention, brought forth several lengths of the aforesaid Venetian sail cloth that she had purchased years back in that providently romantic manner of women who at twenty-one say to themselves, "Some day, when I'm married, I'll have a house with Venetian sail-cloth awnings." Being from farther south than Boston and having a weakness for keeping my feet on rails, I championed the porch. We compromised (we usually do compromise) on a terrace with a porch roof, a terrace with a low Italian wall and a deck above.

A great section of the bank had to be carved out. This exposed the foundations, and the foundations consisted of huge boulders that projected from the house line three feet or more. It looked as though the boulders would have the last laugh. Then Necessity showed her maternal instinct. We invented a way to make those rocks give us a shelf; bricks were laid above them to a

general level, broken to a lower level into steps
as the wall approached the dining-room door.
To-day the lower level serves as sideboard, and
on summer mornings we simply plug in the coffee
percolator and the toaster.

One rock was so enormous that we could not
cover it and the mason suggested our chiseling it
away. This we were loath to do, as he said it
would require the better part of a morning and his
mornings were worth the princely sum of five
dollars each. We puzzled over it for a long time.
Then, in the gloaming of an August night, we
saw that it was n't a rock at all; it bore the shape
of a dog, contentedly lying there. It forthwith
became the mascot and guardian of our property.
We are n't sure of its breed; it has the snout of a
cocker spaniel and the haunches of an Irish terrier.

Red cement gives this roofed terrace a bright
foundation, its brick walls, which are painted
white, tie it to the house, its blue roof throws
down a cooling reflection. The floor being below
the level of the lawn, one has to step up to reach
the garden, or you may merely roll off the broad
top of the wall onto the turf. This broad top
was designed to be fitted with many pillows
and a vast agglomeration of pots filled with
flowers.

One of these days, when we have acquired the
pots and the Scandinavian has been trained to

know a color scheme when he sees one, we shall
try a little futuristic gardening, such as they do in
France. One week, red pots with yellow snapdragons will range down that wall; the next, blue
pots filled with white baby zinnias; then yellow
pots with blue salvia patens. And so on. At
present old brass and copper jugs rescued from
a pushcart on Grand Street do valiant service for
holding armfuls of cut flowers. There may be
more wonderful sights in the world, but I've yet
to see a more subtle blending of color than a
pot-bellied brass jug shined to gold that reflected
here a blue, there a white, there a red, and holding above it massed stalks of "Sulphur King,"
"Mrs. Frank Pendleton," and "Peace" gladiolus.

Since we had made a cosmopolitan porch, we
saw no reason for not furnishing it in a cosmopolitan style. From a collector in Naples, who said
they came from a local church, we had acquired
six rush-bottom chairs. In the worldly style of
Continental ecclesiasticism these chairs were
gaudy with blue paint and gold and arabesques.
To match them we had a dining-table painted,
arabesques and all.

I often wondered what the old church chairs
think of it. At night-time the altar light from
Seville pours down its pious glow upon the scene.
Perhaps there are strange attempts at proselytiz-
ing in the night, vain efforts at conversion. For

mingled with the pious church chairs are chairs of heathen Chinese bamboo, un-Christianly comfortable and just exotic enough to make them interesting. Besides, Moorish tiles are here and the brass pots are Jewish, and the rug thrown over the swing in the farther corner served as arras once in a Turkish harem. I expect to come out there some night and hear that porch reciting the Apostles' Creed! Or will it be *"Om mane padme Om"*?

II

IN the Song of Solomon is a delightful phrase about a certain gentleman who "feeds among the lilies." I have a natural affinity for that young man. His habit of *al fresco* dining is highly commendable. Some day I shall try it — drop into a bed of lilium candidum with my coffee and postprandial cigarette. Until that time I must be content with dining on the porch and gazing at the lilies, these lilies which made Solomon appear anything but the well-dressed man.

At first it gave us a sense of nakedness to dine out on that porch; much the same sensation of being without trousers that a man gets when he stands in front of a long French window. Gradually the clematis clothed us, and now no alimentary bliss is more perfect than that of eating on the porch.

' But of all three meals, these I have an especial
affection for: breakfast, and breakfast *al frèsco*
on an eastward-looking covered terrace is a delight comparable with few delights in the world.

It is among my ambitions (perhaps I shall find
time up here in the country) to write on eating.
That *magnum opus,* which is to be called "A
Handy Guide to Gastronomic Delights," will
speak at length of the varieties of food and the
moods to eat them in; of the dental vegetables,
such as artichokes and asparagus; of learning a
people's *genus* by the sorts of sweets they eat; of
the five and twenty degrees of coffee; of how to
cook curry so that it does n't taste like iodoform;
of the three hundred and thirty national ways of
showing gastronomic satisfaction. It will also
expatiate on the *nuances* of luncheon, the subtle-
ties of tea, and the liturgy of dinner, and a generous share of the space I would reserve for a rhapsody on "Breakfasting as a Fine Art."

A certain wag once said (he has since died) that
there are three things a man should do in private
— washing, marrying, and eating breakfast. This
is a solemn truth. Washing is an act of purifica-
tion, marriage is an act of dedication, and breakfast is an act of contemplation. For the first two
privacy is preferable; to contemplation it is necessary.

One cannot contemplate — and be polite —

surrounded by a family. He must have leisure
and privacy. When a man props a newspaper
before him at breakfast, he is rarely avid for news,
the paper is merely a shield against intrusion.
Wives should understand this. But because many
of us do not appreciate leisure and privacy, we
really do not value a meal devoted to such virtues.

All day we are too busy. At night we are too
tired. It is only in justice to ourselves that we
should lay claim to at least one meal a day. This
is no selfish premise: it is a fact that older people
have proved — leisure and privacy are requisite
for the development of self-respect, discernment,
and poise.

So then —

Luncheon, to business.

Dinner, to the family.

Breakfast, to one's personal thoughts.

That is the perfect day.

Eating breakfast is an art capable of infinite
variations; in fact, to keep its stimulus fresh, both
what we eat and how we eat it should be constantly changed. To look forward to a lifetime
of orange-juice, medium boiled eggs, toast and
coffee, is a dreary prospect. But the unexpected
introduction of bacon or chops, or even oaten
meal, is to the usual menu what a sudden brass
note is in a monotony of plucked strings.

Yet even the unusual can become commonplace. One should therefore make his breakfast fit the occasion. "Heavy" and "light," the only differentiations the ordinary mind recognizes, is a base manner of classifying so variable a subject. Breakfasts should be classed according to place and degree. In my own family (we are two — as you may have suspected) the following kinds are recognized: Ferial, Solemn, Pontifical, English Middle-Class, breakfast in the Bois de Boulogne, and breakfasting among the lilies.

A Ferial breakfast is the usual weekly kind. It is a coffee-and-toast meal, eaten without servitor and in great haste, like the Passover of the Hebrew children, and in much the same style of costume — girded for departure, with our shoes on our feet and our staves in our hands.

A Solemn breakfast is eaten on a holdiay, when there is no need for hurry. We wear the vestments of négligée and follow the ritual of grapefruit, poached eggs, bacon, toast, marmalade, and much coffee. It is usually interspersed with choice bits read aloud from the editorial columns of the newspaper, and Mr. Heywood Broun.

A Pontifical breakfast is possible only when there is company, and comes mostly on Sundays. We are pompously garbed in Sunday clothes, and the servitor wears her best habit. All the dignity of polite manners is observed — the passing of dishes, the mysterious covering and uncovering of

rare viands with silver domes, and that quaint ru-
bric which requires finger-bowls with fruit. It is a
meal, of course; one passes from stage to stage,
from ecstasy to ecstasy, until an end is reached.

These are breakfasts of degrees. The others
are breakfasts of places.[16] For an English Middle-
Class breakfast (which is eaten only in winter)
you draw the table close to an open fire in which
burns cannel coal, keep the coffee-pot on the hob,
have Scotch marmalade instead of jam, tea instead of coffee, and finish with a pipe instead of
a cigarette.

When the first days of spring come before we
move to the country, we have breakfast in the
Bois de Boulogne. The windows of our apartment
in town look over a park, and the trees are close
by. A little table is spread by the window, and
we eat crescent rolls with sweet butter, and have
café au lait — and wish very hard that we were
back in Paris.

Now, I have been married more years than I
would confess — blissfully married — and still,
when breakfast in the Bois is announced, I greet
it with a real thrill of a lark. Still, when I sit down
to a stuffy English Middle-Class breakfast, the
day begins with an unwonted atmosphere. But
it is when I come down of mornings and eat among
the lilies in a sunny corner of that porch that I
feel Nirvana is very close to me.

III

LOCAL custom, not personal preference, decides the manner and kind of breakfasts. Thus, New England, despite its culture and independent ways, persists in that strange excrescence of pie, and even the "Brahmin caste" is addicted to crullers. And this merely because New England is in the pie-belt! Once, in a New England hotel, I was offered the indignity of oyster stew for breakfast — but we shall not speak of that further.

In the South, I am told, breakfast is a great function. As I have never eaten below Mason and Dixon's line I cannot bear witness to this. They have, it is said, a remarkable kind of biscuit which is beaten to a flaky consistency. Moreover, they have a variety of foods irrespective of the days; which is a contrast to New England, where the natives know when Sunday comes because they have codfish balls for breakfast. I am told on good authority that in a well-ordered New England home it is quite impossible to get codfish balls except on Sundays.

The plainsman has bacon because bacon is easily carried, and because he has a fine olfactory appreciation of the aroma of bacon on still prairie air, which is like unto incense. The woodsman eats trout, because it is at hand. He will also

45254A

indulge in blueberry flapjacks — a divine food
not to be spoken of lightly.

The great all-Continental breakfast, including
the Scandinavian, is in the manner of the French,
the variant beverages being coffee or chocolate.
The Russians sometimes drink tea and eat stere-
let — a long, thin fish; but then, the Russians are
given to strange ways. In England breakfast is
a substantial meal of degrees and dignity. And
since we took our early customs from the mother-
land, it was natural that the American breakfast
for the first two centuries should have been a
Gargantuan affair. Americans still talk about
breakfast, but their conversation is an overshad-
owing of the past. It is like their boast of ances-
try. Breakfast was once worth talking about.
We have simply not stopped talking, that is all.

IV

DURING the course of my life I have eaten over
twelve thousand breakfasts. Space and your
patience will permit a recountal of only three.
But these were unforgettable meals.

The first was with a theologian, a white-haired
divine of great repute. He was also very stout,
and ate at a distance from the table. I have
often since wondered why he did not follow the
practice of an earlier divine — Thomas à Kempis
— who, it is related, was so portly that he had a

notch cut in his table in which he could snugly
fit. This divine met me late one night on the
street and deplored the fact that I was staying at
an hotel. Still, as I had taken the room, I must
use it — that was only common sense. But would
I not breakfast with him at his house next morning?

(Right here let me say that an invitation to
breakfast is a mark of real friendship. Never
refuse one.)

I arrived at eight-thirty and went directly to
the dining-room. The table was set for two (he
was a celibate), but it was quite the largest table
for two I had ever seen. A great distance sepa-
rated us. Before we sat down, he said grace —
not one of those mumbled graces that ministers
say when they come to dinner, but a full, man-
sized grace, devoutly spoken. Then I began to
see why he was so thankful — and so stout.

Fruit — endless varieties of it. Oaten meal,
with cream that poured from the pitcher like
molasses. Kippered herring, cooked dry. Bacon
and eggs, the bacon also cooked dry. A huge bas-
ket of assorted rolls. An urn of coffee each. Hot
cakes with maple syrup. Chops and fried potatoes. Stacks of buttered toast, with generous
coatings of bitter marmalade. Cigarettes, pipes,
cigars.

It was well on to eleven when we left the table

— a shoal of empty dishes and books. Books? Yes, countless books. For we talked books, and between courses he would waddle out to his library and return each time with half a dozen volumes. We read from Borrow, Dr. Pusey, Cardinal Manning, Arthur Guiterman, Mrs. Wharton, and several minor British poets.

When the meal was done, he said another long grace. Which leads me to observe that a full breakfast is a meal most devoutly to be thankful for.

The next breakfast was a chimera.

For a month we had been driving our punt — the Why Not? — between the ice-jams of the Amur. At night we would stop and pitch camp and haul the boat high on the banks, for the river froze tight as a drum. Before dawn we awoke, unfroze ourselves, and then unfroze breakfast. But in these latter days the only provisions in the duffle-bag were sour black bread and tea. The prospect was not pleasant, and the nearest village lay forty versts down the river. Eventually we would come to it, but between then and now — black bread and tea. Also, my birthday.

A man should not have a birthday in a Siberian wilderness if he expects to celebrate it. But I could n't help having a birthday, and in a moment of confidence I told my pal the date.

Very early that morning I awoke to smell the

sacramental aroma of bacon. It was unbeliev-
able, but bacon, and you can't very well mistake
it. I stuck my head through the tent-flap. Yes,
it was bacon! He had secreted it against the day
of my celebrating.

"It will be ready in a moment," he announced.

And in a moment it was. I saw the bacon. I
saw him take the four strips of it from the pan
and lay them on a tin plate. The next moment I
saw our fox-terrier dart at that plate. In less
time than I can write it, he wolfed down those
four precious strips. Later in the morning he
came back, licking his chops. We forgave him.

The third was a breakfast to a poet. This was
in the lean days when any meal was a banquet.

The poet had been suffering from ennui and
longed for fresh fields to pasture his Pegasus in.
He tried the ordinary diversions of love and liquor
which the city offered, and then resolved to go
abroad. It was a brave resolve, for he had no
money. But he did possess courage, and it would
take courage to walk aboard a trans-Atlantic
steamer as a stowaway. When detected, as he
felt sure he would be, his passage could be worked
out in heroic pentameters recited for the delecta-
tion of those on board.

These things he confided to us, and we set
about to make his passage easy. We decided on a
farewell breakfast.

A great table was set in the studio. At either end stood immense golden Louis XVI candelabra — borrowed from a rich friend — each with seven tall candles, also borrowed. Midway down one side was placed a kingly chair draped with antique brocade. Sketching-stools and studio flotsam formed the other thirty seats. The guests came in costume, and the models, who had volunteered to serve, wore the scant habiliments of houris.

When the dishes were in place and the shades drawn and the four and ten tall candles ablaze, we marched in, with the poet bringing up the rear and bearing himself nobly, like a great prelate.

Half an hour before noon he departed for his boat. As he left we gave him a dollar bill and a Chinese grammar.

He has since become well known.

X
A CHAPTER ON ANNUALS

BEFORE starting to raise annuals one should consult an actuary's chart to determine approximately how long he has to live. He may also strike an average of the longevity in his family. Figuring on this basis, I calculated that there remained forty years to me, barring automobile accidents, plague, and canned salmon. I could raise annuals for forty years. And since there were about ten hundred and eighty-two different varieties of annuals that I would like to try, I could plan to devote my time to twenty-seven of them each year. When I finished the entire ten hundred and eighty-two, I would know something about annuals. This would bring me past eighty, after which I could just raise my favorites until the summons came.

Then, when I had climbed up to the Pearly Gates and was being interviewed, I might answer the questions after this fashion —

St. Peter: Well, old fellow, what have you done to get into Heaven?

I: I gave a drink to a girl who was low in spirit.

St. Peter: That won't go here. Heaven's Prohibition. What's more we very much dislike puns.

I: Well, then, I tried not to gamble

St. Peter: And according to the records you did n't succeed. What else?

I (*anxious to play my trump card*): Well, I — ah — raised flowers.

St. Peter: That's better. What kind?

I (*proudly*): Annuals, sir. One thousand and eighty-two different varieties of them.

St. Peter (*reflecting*): Ah, yes, annuals! They're a great trouble. You have to plant 'em every year. Well, old fellow, go on inside. You'll find Linnæus and La Notre and Johnnie Appleseed[16] and the rest of the boys over there planting asphodels.

St. Peter would be right. Annuals are an immense bother, and because people don't want to take the bother, they rarely appreciate the real beauty and effectiveness of annuals. These people usually belong to the same benighted group who think that you plant a perennial border once and for all time. To them annuals are just raised to fill in bare spots of the herbaceous border between seasons of perennial bloom. These people may also say, and with some justification, why bother with flowers that give only a short season of bloom, and then leave a bare space in the garden?

In addition to the terror of being bothered is the vivid memory we all have of the days when "bedding" was at its worst; when the carpet dealer of the town had a roll of ageratums, salvia, and asters on his front lawn made up to represent his wares; when lawns were cut up into silly designs and an uninterrupted stretch of turf was rarely seen.   And yet between that hideous extreme and the occasional use of annuals in the herbaceous border lies a happy medium full of garden possibilities.

True, annuals are a necessity in the complete perennial border and some must be raised distinctly for that purpose.   Often they will sow themselves, and one can count on a certain return of that flower and color in that spot year after year.   The original color selection of annuals for a perennial border, however, must be carefully thought out.   Any number of annuals offer a wide color range, and the gardener must visualize his border as a whole before making the final selection.

I wonder if it would n't be possible (in some day approaching the millennium) for seedsmen to furnish a color range with their seeds, much as a manufacturer of fabrics does in showing his wares: when he makes up a new design it is printed in a number of color variations and a "swatch" or collection of clippings showing the color line is provided purchasers to choose from.

A color chart is difficult to work with, since only one very gifted with a color sense can carry a great number of shades and tones in her head. Even working with it in the garden, with the chart in one hand and the flower in the other, I have found more confusing than helpful. It may seem a silly idea, and yet I think it perfectly feasible, for a house like Henderson or Burpee to supply a color "swatch" with its asters or snapdragons, bits of silk matched up the year before to established varieties. With these the gardener could work out her color scheme graphically and to her utmost satisfaction.

Next year I must try this. I will persuade her to collect for me — she who has ways of getting such things — a box of rainbow ribbons and silk-ends, and with these we will make our border charts for each succession of color.

II

ANOTHER method of planting annuals is to have an annual garden in which they can be set out in seemly beds, a bed to a massed variety and color and one or two flowers chosen for each year — a satisfying form of yearly specialization. This year it may be poppies, of which there is a brilliant and varied range, that can be seeded at monthly intervals to prolong the season of bloom; next year the pinks, lavenders, and purples of

annual larkspurs; candytuft the next, and so on.
These would comprise the main flower crop;
other low annuals, of course, being used to give
the beds finish.

Flower specialization of some sort tempts every
true gardener. It is very tantalizing to read about
Sir Michael Foster's great work with iris or Peter
Barr's with narcissus or Joseph Jacobs's with
tulips. Dreaming of their accomplishments, you
make yourself a secret promise that some day
you'll go in for that sort of thing. Alas, what
stars we do hitch our carts to! Foster once
waited eighteen years for the seeds of an Oncocy-
clus iris to germinate! It takes practically seven
years before the characteristics of a new narcissus
are established. We'd be so frightfully old by
that time! Why not get the taste of this sort of
flower exploration by raising annuals and learning as much as you comfortably can about them?
Or, if you are more ambitious, choose a simple
perennial, one that hybridizes easily, such as
columbines. But by growing a good range of
annuals and biennials and keeping notes on them,
you will find an amazing lot of valuable observations in your garden record before the killing
frosts.

A third way of planting annuals — one that is
especially convenient for observation — is to
set them in rows like vegetables and reserve that

part of the garden for cutting. This is our scheme.
The front half of this garden is given to vegetables, the second to annuals, the positions being
reversed from year to year.

An annual nursery of this size — it measures
eighty by seventy-five feet — affords ample room
for trying out many varieties of annuals, dahlias,
gladiolus, and at the farther end some perennials
that we want to study before they find a permanent place. There the range of astilbes is being
studied for color and height and soil acceptance,
there some of the torch lilies will find a temporary
home, and, at wide intervals, are planted one or
two varieties of columbines.[17]

Into this plot the first year went two varieties
of coreopsis, two of clarkia, two of ageratum, ten
of snapdragon, ten of zinnias, ten of asters, a
variety of everlastings and statice for winter
bouquets, and some twenty other annuals that
piqued our curiosity. The second year we reduced the number of kinds and went in for more
color variation, still keeping old favorites that
we could n't do without. Each year, of course,
we shall be playing with some of the novelties.

As years go on, novelties become less and less
a temptation to a gardener, and yet he feels that
he ought to try them out because he might be missing something very well worth while. The temptation is always pressing. Our seedsmen have

inherited from the press agent of the circus the gift
for superlative and glowing descriptions. Harken
to this seductive rhapsody on a new cucumber:
"It is dark-skinned, very handsome in shape,
most prolific, and of splendid flavor. It has hardly
any neck, but a nice sloping shoulder." Could
Robert W. Chambers do better?

III

THERE is no especial secret in raising annuals, one
merely has to have a hot bed and a cold frame, and
time. Also to gain the utmost satisfaction, he
should have a generous disposition. From our
early spring plantings come abundant plants to
fill the annual rows, slip into the herbaceous
border where they often self-sow and thus take
care of themselves, and give away to neighbors.
At the end of each year there is an accumulation
of seed which, put up into little packets and prop-
erly labeled, make acceptable Christmas presents.

I only wish we could increase the popularity of
giving garden gifts here in America. It can come
only when enthusiasm for gardening has become
a more universal and persistent passion. In
England a gift of seeds or plants is cherished;
here, one has to write a little note and explain
such a gift. But when you do find a real gardener
— how such gifts are appreciated! How they are
treasured against their day of planting!

Personally, I would rather have a dozen of those new Chinese lily bulbs — the yellow, white, brown, and pink Regale — than the smartest cravat on the market, and the generous soul who would endow my garden with some sturdy new lilacs, instead of trying to endow me with another silk umbrella, would win my eternal gratitude. There must be many a bride who would prefer a garden started for her instead of the accustomed string of pearls from the fond and extravagant parent — a rose garden, say, laid out with little stone paths converging to a sundial; or a perennial border planted for a succession of her favorite flowers and colors, from the first peep of the crocus to the last chrysanthemum of fall.

To have a flower in a friend's garden is not uncommon; to have a flower in an enemy's garden — what possibilities!

I have a hope that some day American garden-lovers will correspond with others in various parts of the world, the way stamp collectors do, exchanging seed and, where customs regulations permit, plants. A common interest in such gentle and beautiful things as flowers would accomplish more than the mandates of a dozen Leagues of Nations. ("And the leaves of the Tree were for the healing of Nations.") I may still distrust the Germans, with the war so fresh in the mind, but I think that I would feel a little differently about them if a slip sent me from a German garden-lover's rose tree were blossoming by my front steps to-day.

It would be feasible for our flower society bulletins to publish names of American and foreign flower-lovers who would be willing to correspond — some one in Australia, for example, to write me of his experiences with Japanese iris, some one in Greece to say how his poppies grow. . . . This international gardening is worth a thought.

IV

IT was from an English correspondent that I learned a somewhat unorthodox way of planting annuals. Instead of the more common square or oblong bed planting, devoted to one or two kinds as suggested above, or instead of planting in drifts, he takes a long border and divides it criss-cross into lozenges, a kind to each lozenge and with occasional grasses to give foliage and height variation.

A pink-and-red scheme he worked out consisted, in the back row, of sweet peas, Lavatera splendens rosea, pink cosmos, and annual and Shirley red poppies. In the next row of lozenges, coming toward the front, purple larkspur, dark blue comet asters, salvia patens, cornflower, nigella Miss Jekyll, blue convolvulus, blue larkspur, purple-and-gold salpiglossis, light-blue comet asters, lilac scabiosa, purple annual poppies, and purple larkspur. In the middle row, pink snapdragons, crimson godetia, grasses, rose godetia, pink Shirley poppies, pink snapdragons, grasses again, carmine snapdragons, grasses, salmon phlox Drummondi, and pink snapdragon. The front row is of lozenges and half-lozenges — viscaria cærulea and pink linaria, Gilia capitata and pink clarkia, ageratum and red phlox Drummondi, light-blue comet asters and sweet alyssum, Brachycome iberidifolia and dwarf pink phlox Drummondi, blue and pink Nemesia, Phacelia lampanularia and gypsophila elegans, blue salvia and pink stocks, Nemophila insignis grandiflora and pink clarkia, purple verbena and salmon clarkia, dark-blue asters and deep-red snapdragons. The bed is about fifty feet long. It can as easily be planted to a yellow-and-orange or a blue-and-purple scheme.

The use of grass in such a border is very interesting, and gives a stimulating note to annual plantings. Stipa pennata or feather grass, with the delicate, silvery white feathery plumes; the curious Briza gracilis and cloud grass, agrostis, would afford pleasing variations of foliage.

There are in this list some annuals that deserve more attention by American gardeners. All can be found in our catalogues. Clarkia is known to us, but not too well known. It has a delightful manner of growth both in the loose elegans and in the clustered pulchella types. The color range is very pleasing, running from vivid crimson rose and salmon scarlet through delicate pinks and rose to white. Brachycome iberidifolia or the Swan River Daisy, listed by a number of our seedsmen, is a native of West Australia, and the flowers are dainty and small, giving a good summer bloom that ranges from a soft mauve of "Summer Beauty" to a clear blue in "Little Blue Gem" and back to the white. Viscaria is quite hardy, growing about one foot high, and can be had in carmine, rose pink, bright-blue, and white. In Scotland the Nemesia is almost as popular as the nasturtium is with us and is almost as easily grown, being hardy. The pale yellow is a lovely delicate shade and the color range includes rose, pink, white, orange, crimson, and scarlet. In the hybrid or dwarf strains there is also a blue-and-white bi-color variety. Nemophila, a hardy annual, affords delightful white, spotted, and lavender varieties, together with white, bright-blue, and purple variations. Gilia capitata, an annual type used in the English garden, bears attractive light-blue flowers in globular heads; the Tricolor types, lavender, white, and rose; the Nivalis, a delicate scented snow-white. The Coronapifolia, scarlet crimson, is a half-hardy biennial.

V

To the professional landscape architect all this chatter about color in the garden sounds rather amateurish; in fact, many of our landscapists are apt to snort when you venture to mention such matters. Color, in the garden, it appears, is merely a plaything for sentimental women.

American landscaping suffers at present from a serious attack of Naturalizitis. Wild gardening and massed shrubbery and tree-moving are its present-day passions. Its ideal is to hedge in the view and make one thing blend into another. Because of this the herbaceous border has lost some of its professional popularity and the annual garden is looked upon as the vagary of an unknowing mind.

I number dozens of these landscapists, male and female, among my friends and I sympathize with their endeavors. They hope to make a new heaven of these United States and a new earth — and they will do it eventually. They can see a garden as a whole; they can, by very simple changes, give a property unity of design and unusual interest. To them is greatly due the honor for making America a country of beautiful gardens which it is becoming, our English cousins to the contrary. But — and here I set down both feet — I think it a great mistake to run to extremes in garden design. Wild gardening and massed shrubbery can as easily become fads, as short-vamp shoes and henna hair-wash. When fads run to extremes there is inevitably a reaction, and there will be a reaction to these.

Spare us, O spare us the stiff beds of annuals! Spare us the iron stag browsing in concentric circles of anæmic pink and baby-blue asters; But let us have gardens where balance is maintained, where wild gardening will find a place because it is logical and the site demands it, where shrubbery will be used with fastidious reserve, where the herbaceous border will cease from troubling and the annuals be at rest!

XI

A MATTER OF LITTLE BOOKS

I

I 'VE always had a prejudice against men who put down figures in little account books. It is the sort of habit you see lauded in magazines devoted to the life stories of twenty-dollar-a-week clerks who become millionaires. This practice is precisely the sort of thing that devastates a man's character; it makes him a millionaire and nothing else

On the other hand, I have the deepest affection for men and women who put their thoughts down in little books — not the Margot Asquith sort of diary, the washing of dirty linen on the front porch, but the Eugénie Guérin sort, the Amiel sort, the Private-Papers-of-Henry-Ryecroft sort. We have too few of them nowadays, too few people thinking, speculating, meditating, too few willing to take the trouble of writing down what they do think.

I also have a deep admiration for the people who make up private anthologies. Like Marcella Burns, the fairy godmother of bookselling in America. For years Marcella (as radiant a creature as a Killarney rose) has been clipping things out of magazines and newspapers and copying them to put in what she called her "Hospital Book." Whenever a friend gets laid up, Marcella calls and leaves her book with the patient. She claims to have converted seventeen hard-boiled business men to the enjoyment of poetry by this method of feeding them beautiful verse while they were helpless. Her Hospital Book is to Chicago what the Mother of Kazan ikon is to Moscow — carried about to sick beds to save desperate cases.

Now, it is conceivable that a business man sick in bed may find amusement and interest in a tabulation of figures; there are such. Heaven help them! They need all the help that Heaven can give. But it is more conceivable that a private anthology will cure what doctors cannot. To a garden-lover a book especially designed for her would mean an entirely new lease on life.

Acting on Marcella's (every one knows her as that) suggestion I have begun a Gardener's Hospital Book. It is an agglomeration of clippings from French, German, Dutch, English, and American seed catalogues and garden magazines, copied-out paragraphs from gardening-books, together with poetry and prose dealing with various picturesque and inspiring phases of gardening and country life. These are arranged according to subjects in a loose-leaf binder and can be added to as new material comes to hand.

At first an anthology of this sort is bewildering to read; it is, in many instances, an "experience meeting" of gardeners, a "testimonial meeting," and their experiences and testimonials may differ so radically that the reader is confused. That, of course, is the criticism which can be made of reading too many gardening-books — one says one thing, another says another. But by getting the consensus of opinion, as the parliamentary works express it, a general average can be struck. Also, the radically different experience of some one gardener may be precisely the sort of experience you should have. As a working proposition, apart from its pathological uses, this garden anthology has unquestioned merit. Taken together with Bailey's Encyclopædia it gives a full survey of the gardening world. I recommend it to garden-lovers. Make up your own hospital book. Try it on yourself when you are out of sorts with the world. It is a potent factor in recovery.

II

EVERY one, of course, should keep a garden record and every one seems to have a different method in keeping it. The card-index system, with a different card for each kind of flower or plant, is the simplest style. Write or type on the top of the card the botanical and common names, the original habitat, color, height and type of foliage, the general type of treatment that authorities suggest, its location in your garden, and when you planted it there. Below this leave space for monthly observations.

A round of the garden once a week, after the beds are weeded and the general work is through, gives opportunity to make a survey, count blossoms, and watch color. At the end of the month these general observations, which have been taken down in a rough garden notebook, can be cast up on the cards.

These cards should be prepared at the same time you are making out your seed order for the new year or when you are contemplating changes in the garden. Don't attempt to compile them in the spring; there is n't time. The fall or late winter are the best seasons.

An additional piece of data can be added, as years go on, to these cultural facts; that is, the combination of this plant with others. Here again we strike the bewilderment of reading many gardening-books. Gardening authorities are constantly trying out new combinations of color, form, and foliage. The beginning gardener should, as I advised previously, work out her own combinations. Don't become a slave to too much advice. What the cooks can do to the soup can as readily happen to the garden. But, having tried out her own combinations, then let the gardener tabulate her own and the experiences of others; let her set down what Miss Jekyll and Mrs. King and Mrs. Shelton and Mrs. Ely, what Wister and Thomas and McFarland and Havemeyer, have tried out.

You will probably be very ancient when you finally arrive at the garden rule which completely satisfies you. If you never do arrive, you can only hope that in the next incarnation you will be placed in more easy garden circumstances.

At first sight such a bothersome thing as keeping these cards may appear to defeat the end of gardening, to tire one of the hobby. Of course, it should not be overdone; neither should the collecting of stamps or the drinking of good whiskey. It is just as necessary to be temperate about gardening as it is to be temperate about eating, drinking, sleeping, reading, praying, playing, working, and loafing. One may, if he chooses, merely take gardening as a casual pastime. The chances are that he will not. Once he has learned its joys, he will want to go deeper and deeper into it. And there is a reason, which I shall permit Leonardo da Vinci to express. That old master, who said many wise things, once wrote: "The knowledge of a thing breeds love of it. The more exact the knowledge the more fervent the love."

It is difficult, in the rush and competition of modern American life, to spend as much time as one might wish over garden records. It is desirable, however, that as much time as can be spared be devoted to them. You can't do it if you are spending most of your time at the local country club. You can't do it if you are jockeying for alleged social position in your town. You can't do it if you are n't much at home. These things, like collecting, presuppose a love of home, that home which is a part of you as you are a part of it. That's the whole sum and substance of this argument, that is the suggestion of this chapter, that is the testimony of these pages.

III

FROM the time I was a small lad I can remember my father (may his cellar last many years!) working over a big scrapbook that he kept in his library. Every now and then I would find him with shears and paste, sticking into it pictures cut from magazines. One day he confided to me what it was all about. It was the book of the house he would build, when he has money enough. There the old dear had saved every conceivable kind of architectural detail — roof, doorway, window, chimney, path, and façade. Pity the architect to whom he took that book!

And yet precisely that sort of thing is being

done by thousands of people in America to-day. And it is one of the most potent factors in laying the foundation for a right national life. The house scrapbook is a book of dreams. Most of them will never be realized, but they represent the measure of taste and desire in the minds of people who believe in the home.

During the past eight years my energies have been devoted to the editing of a magazine in which the building of houses, the decoration of rooms, and the making and maintenance of gardens are the three main interests. In that short time I have witnessed a gradual increase and improvement of taste in America, a growing interest in the creating of beautiful homes and gardens. It has been due to an increasing desire on the part of the American people to strengthen the home. It has been brought about partly by just such simple little things as house scrapbooks. To-day the interest in these subjects is widespread. A well-decorated home is as vital to-day to a woman in Dallas, Texas, as it is to the woman on Park Avenue, New York.[18] I feel sincerely that this is an earnest of very good things to come. The desire to have a home, the act of having one; the desire to make that home more beautiful each year, the accomplishment of this desire; the dream of having a garden, the attainment of that dream — these things are the bulwarks of a people.

IV

FORGIVE me; I let that idea run away with my plan for talking on house records. There is still another to mention. I refer to the journal, the diary.

They say that ever since Mrs. Asquith's diary was published, London book-sellers have had a run on diaries. Every one is scribbling down what she thinks of every one else.

Like as not something of that sort is going on in select American circles. The great mass of people have a penchant for reading overheard conversations. They love their bits of scandal the way scrubwomen used to love (and perhaps still do) their nips of gin. And the people who write diaries of this sort are usually natural gossips. Pepys and Evelyn, the great forerunners of these modern diarists, seemed to find in their diaries an outlet for their wagging tongues. In a previous era to our own, gentlewomen found diaries an outlet for their affections; they lived through many a lurid affair of the heart in the pages of their journals. It was safe and sane; afforded all the excitement of romance without the headache of scandal.

My suggestion that garden enthusiasts keep a journal is based on very much these same principles — a journal will prove an outlet for thoughts, satisfy the craving to write (which all too many of us think we can do), and spare our friends the bother of having to listen to us. Mind you, I am no cynic, but I have a peculiar dislike for the enthusiastic gardener who takes the seat beside me on the commuter's special and insists on talking all the way to town about how wonderful his garden grows. If only that man wrote it down in a book, he might be more inclined to leave me in peace. Besides, *my* garden is usually far better than his.

I confess, unashamedly, that I have kept a journal off and on for years. It is a scrapbook of thoughts and impressions, a record of varying experiences, opinions, prejudices, hates, dislikes, and affections. As I turn over its pages now, I am reminded of what a parson once replied to me. He had been attached for many years as chaplain to a woman's reformatory. I remarked that such a place should furnish him with many interesting human documents. "Yes, they are human documents," he replied, "but very few of them are worth reading; their authors are mainly defectives." Most of my journal is defective; its thoughts half-baked, its prejudices unfounded.

I found that so long as I lived in a city, it was a journal of people — what people said and did and were like. When I acquired these seven acres more or less, its topics radically changed. People *per se* lost much of their interest. Fewer and fewer times did I record the quips some minor poet threw off at luncheon, and the merry jests of Charles Hanson Towne. What did impress me, and what I did start to set down, was an entirely new and different set of impressions. Whereas I used to regard the sentimentalizing of Amiel as watery stuff for a man to write — just the sort of thing to tickle the sweet tooth of the Victorians — I have arrived at a great respect for that gentleman. Whereas once on a day the journals of Eugénie and Maurice Guérin used to strike me as precisely the sort of thing Matthew Arnold loved to write about, I find myself turning back to those two delightful diaries with a distinct sense of relief after the bucolic photographic novels of young America.

Joyce Kilmer (may he now have joined the valiant band of Keats and Shelley!) once wrote me a poem called "Main Street," and it wound up in Heaven. Too many of our Main Streets wind up in the gutter; too many of them are simply records of the drear monotony that makes small-town and country life, when abused and overdone, end in inbreeding, degeneracy, and discontent.

V

I CONTEND that too much of country life can drive a man to homicide. The bitter grind that one finds on many farms is responsible for those hideous country crimes one reads in almost every morning's paper. The city man who takes up country living is no exception to this peculiar spiritual devastation that too much contact with the soil can wreak. He must always be on his guard lest he go out fantee.

I remember once crossing the trail of a man in the little Siberian town of Stretensk in Trans-Baikalia. He was an American mining engineer, college bred, married, and a father. His work took him to a desolate country. As the years passed, he lost more and more of his breeding, his contact with civilized things, his desire to live in a civilized fashion. He had gotten down to busk sandals, a sheepskin coat, and a native wife, and even his mother tongue was fast slipping beyond him. Gone out fantee! They say that, lest he go out fantee, the Englishman will dress for dinner in the middle of a jungle. These are extreme cases. The amateur farmer may feel only a slight touch of this temptation to revert to primitive ways, but however mild the temptation, it is there nevertheless. The same soil which can be cleansing may also grind him down. The same upward whirling of Nature which may take him to the heights may also hurl him into the depths. The disease might be called Ruralomania.

There are many cures for it, and one is to keep

just such a journal of his sentiments and aspirations as Amiel kept, to weep on paper just as
Eugénie Guérin wept, to struggle against the
overwhelming forces of Nature with his pen just
as Maurice Guérin struggled, to survey it at
last placidly, serenely, philosophically as George
Gissing did in "The Private Papers of Henry
Ryecroft."

XII
THE WISDOM OF SITTING STILL

I

In my youthful folly I nursed a vain illusion. I thought that gardening would flood me with a tide of noble and inspiring thoughts. I had a picture of myself hoeing corn of an August afternoon when, suddenly, a blinding light would open up heavenly visions to my eye. I would drop the hoe, run to my desk, and, while the inspiration still burned hot within me, pour forth immortal Maeterlinckian essays on why flowers are intelligent or the loveliness of clouds or the home life of the nuthatch and the purple martin. Alas, no such inspiration came! Gardening meant just perspiration, groans, tired muscles, and unspeakably dirty hands. I tried to meditate, to sit quietly in a shadowed corner cross-legged like Buddha, but the moment I started to contemplate my eye would fall on a weed that I had overlooked, and that would be the end of contemplation. It seemed that all I was to get out of gardening were flowers, vegetables, and thirty pounds less flesh.

The trouble, of course, was that I was overdoing. It had been my habit to start working

about seven in the morning and to keep it up
until the last light faded, then going about with
a lantern to seek and slay cutworms. This made
a strenuous week-end. Add to it labor every
night after a day in the office, and there was
little wonder that my frontal rotundity became
reduced.

This was all very well. I rejoiced in my loss of
flesh. I had attained that slimness when I could
wear a double-breasted coat with impunity — one
of the ambitions of my life. But I was also paying
a heavy price. When, I asked, was my pen to be
quickened by country life? When was I going to
acquire inspiration? After all, there is no use
trafficking with the things that make for the
world's peace, such as flowers and vegetables,
unless one gets from that contact a supply of clear
thoughts and lofty sentiments, a well-spring that
will afford refreshment while passing through the
desert.

Then I attained wisdom. It came in two ways
— by taking off a night in town and by learning
to sit still.

So soon as a man shows a tendency to become
a slave to his garden, to suffer from Ruralomania,
let him pack a night-case and depart for the
nearest city. There let him eat out luxuriously
and riotously with the "boys," let him sit in a
front row orchestra seat, let him sleep in a stuffy

room where he will hear the rattle of mail trucks and the murderous explosion of automobile exhausts. These will keep him awake and make him angry. Being angry, he will start to make invidious comparisons between living in the city and living in the country. Before sleep overcomes him, he will have had enough of the city.

Women are more honest about Ruralomania than men. That is because the wife has not alone to suffer her own but her husband's satiety. Also women recover much more quickly than men, especially if they have small children at home and incompetent servants. The female of the species very quickly and without warning announces the fact that she's had enough of being housemaid, cook, and laundress. She comes down to breakfast dressed in her best, she goes into town on the commuter's special, rushes from one department store to another buying things that she can return as soon as they are delivered, treats herself and a friend to luncheon in a restaurant where they will enjoy being seen, and then inveigles her husband into taking her to an expensive dinner and providing seats for the theater afterwards. If she does this once in two weeks, or even only once a month, she will never long for the bright lights permanently. Nor will her husband.

II

As for sitting still, that is another matter.

From the first week the spade could go into the ground until this hour — this house of abundant blossom and promising fruit — there was no cessation in our work. We had plunged into the country lustily, like good swimmers. Hands that were soft with office work became calloused and brown. We learned the swift anger of the hoe and the measured rhythm of the scythe. Steadily we pursued our war on weeds and pests. Where once lay dun fields now range the orderly rows. Peonies and iris splash their colors along the border. The shadows lengthen across a velvet lawn, close-cropped and weeded.

Indoors, the house glistens with fresh paint and the foot sinks deliciously into new carpets. We began this second year with the entire house cleansed and rejuvenated. The walls look down upon more new furniture. The windows are prim with fresh-laundered curtains.

Each day a great deal is done — a great deal more than we thought could be done. Then, as dusk closes down, we stop amid the chaos of our labors to learn the wisdom of sitting still. We had not known this the first year nor even dreamed that such wisdom could be vouchsafed us. Having passed the neophyte stage, we were ready to make our real profession in the order of country-lovers.

Sitting still is the first requisite of repose. One gains strength by it, as Isaiah counsels. So much is accomplished by sitting down and sitting still — the actual, physical act of sitting. Visualize the Feeding of the Five Thousand — the seething, zealous mob, hungry and tired, the two small loaves and five small fishes. It may be a far cry from that Galilean hillside to this hillside in New England, and yet the miracle did not happen until the men were made to sit down. And the miracle of repose was not vouchsafed us until we, too, had sat down.

Repose is as necessary to the soul as sleep is to the body. Every life, even the busiest, should have its moments of repose; in fact, the busier the life, the more repose is required.

Some find repose in the solitary walk along the country road, others in the walk home through the crowded streets after the day's work. It is difficult to say in which he is more alone. Still others must wait until the household quiets down or the office closes. Whatever the time or place, the first requisite is that one be at least mentally sitting still. Although the body may be functioning subconsciously — as in walking — the mind must be made to sit down and sit still.

The second requisite for repose is that one be

alone, that he enjoys detachment, that most
aristocratic of all aristocratic attitudes, as Remy
de Gourmount calls it. It may not be possible to
be physically alone, yet by the very act of will
one can close the physical senses and shut out
distractions.

Sitting still tends toward simplicity, and simplicity as Thomas à Kempis says, doth tend
toward God.

For once we have attained this simplicity, once
we are shut off from the world, then do the windows and doors of the soul's house open on that
more lovely Day Spring — as a housewife, after
a storm, opens doors and windows to let in clean
air and fresh sunshine. Then does the Sun of
Righteousness spread across the floor of that being and the threshold know His footfall for which
it has awaited.

The wisdom of sitting still becomes Divine
Wisdom when we permit this inflowing. We have
done our part: we have sat down and sat still.
We have awaited It as one awaits a guest. The
household of the soul is quiet against His coming
Sursum corda! We lift up our hearts. *Cor Cor
dium!* Our heart is flooded with His love!

The soul, said St. Bernard, is a capacity for the
infinite. The fluid of the Holy Spirit accommo-
dates itself to a man's capacity and fashion. One
does not have to be a saint to have it fill his vessel

up to the brim, nor rich in spiritual experience
nor learned in matters theological. It stimulates
each man in the manner of his being and work in
life.

So comes Divine Wisdom to each man in his
moments of repose. It may not be what he expects or what at that time he thinks he needs, but
It will approach each in his own fashion, in his
own circle and temperament, on his own peculiar
plane.

Nor, indeed, may It always stimulate him to
religious aspirations. As if in very abnegation of
Himself, the Divine Beauty hides His face from
our beholding and turns our eyes to His handi-
work instead — to the surge of music, the swirl
of clouds, the heave and roll of the sea, the singing of a bird, the heavy odor of grapes in autumn,
the tingle of cool air on a crisp morning, even to
our purpling dusks at the end of the day's work
in the garden.

> Some think Creation's meant to show Him forth;
> I say it's meant to hide Him all it can.

It would be silly to think repose merely an end
in itself. We rest — but the Divine Stimulus
functions only when we apply it. Feeling it active within him, a man hurls himself into the
next moment's contacts. He is driven by a force
more compelling than any on earth. It sends him,

if for but one short moment, to the very frontiers of the world. He sees — and we have seen it through the dusk on our New England hillside — the faint, far horizon of a Celestial Country.

III

WE all possess, to a greater or less degree, a spiritual appetite, and gardening is one of the ways in which it can be gratified. No man can work conscientiously close to the soil without being caught in the upward swirl that marks the rhythm of Nature. It may fling him into the arms of God or hurl him into the depths of a divine despair. But he cannot resist it. Let Socrates protest that country places and trees could teach him nothing. Poor fellow, after all he may have drunk the hemlock for a final anodyne against satiety! The Spaniard Fray Luis de Leon has made a nicer distinction: "It may be that in the cities one learns to speak better," he says, "but delicacy of feeling belongs to the country and the silent places."

With each of us this delicacy of feeling finds a different expression. One gardener may turn pantheist and seek the old gods in bush and woody grove; another may read in the disciplining of the soil the stern negation of the Puritans; another may see in the delphinium's blue the trailing hem of the Virgin's robe; the mystics read the

Trinity into every three-leafed plant and saw the
bloody crown in every bramble thicket.

IV

WHILE purely religious sentiment does not necessarily follow on close living with the soil, it is
difficult to conceive of a man or woman being
pachyderm to the traditions of the soil, those traditions that reach down into the race roots of
mankind.

The traditions of the soil and the things that
go with it have abided when others are forgotten.
The shape of farming implements, for example.
The modern steel plough has no different shape
from that used ten centuries ago, because its
purpose is the same. We turn the same sort of
furrows to-day that Horace did on his Sabine
farm. I remember seeing in Siberia two farmers
in adjoining allotments working with ploughs
that showed these extremes. One was the native
sholka, carved from the gnarled limb of a tree,
the other a brand-new implement fresh from the
International Harvester Works near St. Peters-
burg. They both had the same shape of coulter.
In the same way the sickle has always had about
the same peculiar formation. I've yet to find the
latest American design, the one with the blade
at almost right angles from the handle, any improvement. The rake, the spade, the fork are all

about the same. It would seem as though these tools that go with the soil had been made once and for all.

I have a theory that this is the sort of thing men cling to. In a world turned upside down, with confidence shattered and fanatics battening on the corpse of dead hope, men hunger for touch with those things that have defied the mutations of time.

Even as abiding is the law of the soil. In the garden Nature to-day is, as she has always been, at once both friend and foe. Weeds serve the same purpose that they did in the age of the patriarchs — the gardener is eternally uprooting them, and in uprooting them he cultivates the soil and gives his crop a chance to thrive.

Just as the life of man must be disciplined if it is to be brought to fruition, so must the garden know the discipline of shears and the binding of cords. Something of the painful discipline that makes saints and martyrs makes the exquisite flower and the sturdy plant. The vine is cut back so that it will bear abundantly. The humble celery must suffer entombment in earth to become white against the day of its harvest resurrection. Lashed to a stake, like Joan of Arc, the consuming spirit of a rose blossoms into unforgettable loveliness and the gladiolus strains flaming arms to the sky.

The inexorable and inviolate law of the soil remains when other laws are swept aside. Obedience to it is what works the magic in men's souls so that they are caught upward in Nature's encircling. The radicals of the world may theorize on liberty, statesmen may talk of this and councils argue of that; the gardener knows only one law — discipline. He cuts off twenty blossoms to give perfection to one. Quite unwittingly he applies to his garden the Nietzschean principle of the Superman.

From start to finish he must impose discipline — but also, he himself is subject unto it. Patiently he watches the metamorphosis of seed to flower. Vigilantly he protects it against pest and the fury of the elements. The first frost reduces most of his flowers to a mess of withered stalk and blackened blossom. The second and the third annihilate it altogether. He who has disciplined the soil and laid obedience on Nature that his endeavor bear greater fruit, lo, he himself then knows the discipline of winter!

XIII

THE TYRANNY OF CLOSETS AND BOOKS

I

BETWEEN women and closets is a definite and marked affinity. Something in the tissue make-up of a woman finds sympathetic relationship with the make-up of a closet. Perhaps one of these days Mr. Havelock Ellis or W. L. George can be persuaded to turn upon this problem their searching comprehension of feminine traits.

The feminine person who guides my destinies in this present incarnation gave me, shortly after marriage, a strange clue to the secret of this closet complex. She asked me to get her several large, strong clothes boxes. After much trouble I managed to procure them. Then my woes commenced.

She calls it "regulating." It consists in taking things from one box or drawer and putting them into another. It invariably attacks her on holidays, when I do not have to go to the office and count on having a quiet day at home to write. She will start by looking for a handkerchief, the casual handkerchief that any one could pick from a top bureau drawer blindfolded. The handkerchief will suggest a piece of lace some-

where. She searches for the lace, and in searching
for it must turn over a pile of underwear. Turning over the pile of underwear gives her the notion
that perhaps the underwear might be handier in
the second drawer where the blouses are. Shifting the blouses from the second drawer down to
the third, gives her a like notion about her stockings. In a few minutes she'll be engrossed in
"going to Jerusalem" with all her personal habiliments and mine, too.

Then I am called from a story that is swimming
along to help take down those boxes from the
top shelf. She spreads them out in piles around
my desk and begins shifting the contents of one
into the other and *vice versa*. Apologetically she
asks me to print new labels, and, seeing that the
day is ruined for me, I acquiesce with Christian
meekness.

You see, I made a great mistake the first time
she had an attack of regulating. It was at the
beginning of our married life. In a frivolous moment I wrote my labels in free verse. Of course,
I've had to do it ever since. Things like this —

> This doth contain,
> Much to my soul's wonder and her amazement,
> None else than
> The relic of last winter's purple tricotine skirt
> And three silken knickers, rosy as the dawn,
> A brassière with lace and
> My immortal flannel trousers.

By nightfall on regulating days I've usually out-amyed Amy Lowell, Ezra Pound, and all the Imagists. The story forgotten, I turn my wits to writing epitaphs that read after this fashion —

Beneath This Lid Lyeth
Until The Last Day
A Velvet Evening Frock
of Pale Blue
Ruined By A Taxi Door
Born 1919 — Died 1919

"And They Rent Their Garments."

II

THIS passion for taking things out of one box and putting them into another, of shifting underwear from the lowest to the second drawer, is a feminine weakness that can be cured only by giving a woman an unconscionable number of closets and boxes to play with. I was quite willing to fill every corner of that country house with closets, if only I be spared writing free-verse labels. There were plenty of closets in it — large, ample closets enough for a family of six. Then one day, when everything had been finished and the carpenter was a dead memory, and his bills had finally attained the oblivion of being paid, then she came to me.

"Carissimo," she said, "I want to do something."

"You may, Madame," I replied — knowing that I might as well.

"I am going to get the carpenter to put in some more closets."

"And will I have to write epitaphs for them?" I asked.

"No, Carissimo, only cheques."

And so the carpenter was with us once again.

I had hoped that I would be spared a closet. In my own sanctum — Orphant Annie's Room — I had escaped the discipline of orderliness, my manners were free and uncontrolled. That old sea-chest did valiant service. Now I was to be uplifted. I came home one night to find a closet in the corner of my room. It was a regular, full-grown closet with a shelf where hats were to be laid away in orderly manner, hooks, a shelf for boots, and innumerable coat-hangers. I told her that her thoughtfulness touched my heart. I hope I shall never be held accountable for those words.

The principle she worked on in this attack was: see a corner, build a closet. The leaves in Valambrosa were but a handful compared with the closets she created. Some were complicated, some quite simple, some real works of art and ingenuity. There was the closet in the Blue Room.

I knew this Blue Room puzzled her because, on several occasions, I had found her standing there gazing at the corner opposite the door which is at

the head of the stairs. Up this corner ran a pipe
from the bathroom below. It was a modest pipe,
not too noticeable, although silvered with banana-
oil paint. Had the house been new, of course, that
pipe would have been concealed in the wall. She
spent days puzzling how to make that pipe look
unlike a pipe. The solution came at last.

The pipe was boarded in and a closet built
around it, a closet in an angle, taking up very
little room and yet commodious. It has three
sets of doors — a little set opening on a hat shelf,
a second set for a long cupboard to accommodate
clothes, a third for the shoe shelf. When the carpenter had made these doors, I carried them to
town, protesting every step of the way, and delivered them into the hands of a painter, the same
who had made the morning-glories grow up the
bedposts and over the front of the bureau.
Several weeks later I carried them back again.
Looking at them to-day I often wonder why
people talk so much about the Sistine Chapel.
Those panels are lovely with delicate tints;
the flowers have a similitude that would deceive
even a honey-searching bee. Every now and then
I go into the Blue Room just to gaze at them.
And I come out thinking what a lucky fellow I
am — having a wife and a closet like that.

But the real achievement, the ultimate attainment of her closet ambitions, is found in the

bathroom. It is a trick closet, such as Houdini uses on the stage — little doors and large doors and sliding doors and doors that turn out to be drawer fronts. It is built on the Biblical principle of there being one glory of the moon and another of the sun and another of the stars.

Here are shelves for ordinary sheets and shelves for company sheets, compartments for common blankets and compartments for special blankets, sections for hand towels, guest towels, bath towels, bath sheets, face cloths, and a ventilated shelf where soaps can dry and harden. Here are drawers for boot-cleaning equipment, and a cupboard for the vacuum machine and another for brooms, brushes, dusting-cloths, and whisks, with a compartment below it for brass polish, floor-rags, and all the other submerged tenth of domestic management.

I know not what hours of study and figuring went into that closet; I only know that a man could not have designed it. It is frankly the work of a woman, a woman in many ways as complicated as the closet she has created. I add it to the wonders that puzzled Solomon.

III

But if she has her closets, I have the disposition of the books, and I made it a rule that there should be no room without them. A bedroom without books, of course, is inconceivable. There should always be a Bible in the bathroom. The kitchen library I have spoken of before and the ideal country-house library. The morning-room library had to be selected according to the bindings — something that did n't clash with Adam green. So I chose small bibelots decorative on the outside and entertaining within. Mostly French, these. The French have a knack for making little books that delight the eye.

When it came to putting a row of books out on the porched terrace, I met with opposition. Women seem to be more appreciative of the liturgy of a meal than men are — the rubrics of how to sit and serve and hold the napkin and manipulate the fork. I had a notion — I still have it — that a meal should be spread out over a long period, and reading books aloud makes this possible.

In the Drinking Age one could linger at the table until he was dragged from beneath it. This habit was started by the sporting bishops and writers of "Ye-Old-Cheshire-Cheese" period of literature. At a sale of antiques recently I saw an item that belonged to this era, an eloquent document of long dining. It was a drunkard's chair. The arms were on hinges and folded back, so that when the bibulous one had finished his last glass, the servants came, folded back the

arms, and lifted him off to bed. O worthy men!
O noble days! At Berne there was once a law,
I've read, against sitting at table for more than
five hours, and at Basle 10 A.M. to 6 P.M. were the
legal limits set for the midday meal.

Once on a day it was possible for a man to sit
for hours over cordials. It may be that he will
now sit for an equally long time over his coffee.
But there is a simpler and more effective way of
spreading a meal out over several hours; read a
book.

Within easy reach of our terrace dining-table
is a row of books of the sort that go well with
meals. There is the historic pocket edition of
Charles Lamb. Splashed across two pages of the
essay on "The Illustrious Defunct" are coffee
stains made in a low den on the Bolshaia, in Ir-
kutsk, when my friend Digby pounded the table
over a ribald Siberian jest and made the cups
dance. "The Genteel Style in Writing" was once
held open by a fork in a Blagowestchensk hotel —
you can see the fork's impression to this day where
the lout of a waiter pressed it in by setting a
bottle on top of the open book. When dinner is
going dangerously fast, I take down my smudgy-
faced Lamb or the other tid-bit volumes and read
aloud. The meal is enriched and lengthened by
the book and the book made more memorable
by the meal.

There is quite a large body of this eating literature, and in using it one should choose the volume according to one's guests and the occasion itself. A book containing short pieces is desirable, and the more obscure or forbidden or forgotten the better. For the middle-aged there are the less read parts of Leigh Hunt, and perhaps Neil Lyons or John Donne for a cordial. When the minister comes to dine, read from Coventry Patmore's "The Rod, The Root and The Flower." You can be pretty safe that he never heard of it. Lusty young men might prefer the drinking-ballads of Theodore Maynard, or John V. A. Weaver's "In American." Pompous old fgentlemen could be made to unbend with Calthrop's "Et Cetera"; you could impress them with Erasmus' "Folly," or open the eyes of the worldly minded with the pseudo-naughtiness of D. W. Lawrence. Periodicals, too, make excellent literary beverages, especially obscure periodicals from foreign lands.

Now, it is a pleasing sight to see a man beat out the rhythm of a poem with a serving-spoon. There is something jovially wholesome in sending a page from Lithgow's "Rare Adventures" flooding down the table to wash away all the small talk before it.

I knew a man once who galvanized a dinner party by reading excerpts from Rabelais, ex-

cerpts which he attributed to the Reverend Percy
Stickney Grant.

This is the real music one should have with his
meals. This is the ultimate ecstasy of the table.
Whether one eats ferially or in great pomp, it is
the Nirvana of platter pleasures to butter one's
bread with a book and wash down one's victuals
with bumpers of roaring verse.

IV

Now that I am on the subject of books, I must
bear witness to the peculiar manner in which gardening estranged me from them.

Once on a day books were my passion. I
bought them when I could n't afford to, and read
them when I should have not. I could not imagine sitting idle for ten minutes without picking
up a volume and browsing in it. What the books
were about did n't seem to make much difference: I could start off with something on Phila-
delphia Colonial architecture and find myself
engrossed with it. I would dabble my mental
toes in the smooth waters of "Chats on Old
Furniture" and soon be up to the neck. Or it
might be Evelyn Underhill on some obscure
Italian mystic or Royal Cortissoz on some ob-
scurer Italian painter. Books, just books. The
fact that it was between covers seemed to be the
guiding influence.

And then I took up gardening.

I do not pretend to understand how the metamorphosis came about; I only know that in some mysterious way I was released from the tyranny of books. After an hour playing with seedlings in a cold frame I have n't the slightest desire to turn a page. Books seem so utterly inane, so footless, and the reading of them vanity of vanities. Even at this moment the shelves range above me from ceiling to floor. There is a set of Barrie that would fit this mood to a T. Here are George Herbert's poems and the slim volumes of Francis Grierson's essays. In days past I would turn to such books with a sense of great refreshment, knowing that they would give me stimulus and quicken my thought. Now I have no desire to touch them. Other thoughts fill me.

Across the study window reaches the white arm of the cherry, tossing its blossoms in the spring air . . . up in the barn the Scandinavian is mixing poison for spray to wash down these limbs when the petals begin to fall . . . Those new strains of columbine that came in last week from Boston have been planted in the special columbine seed-bed . . . My neighbor up the road has promised me, on his word of a gentleman, that he will let me have two loads of manure next Wednesday . . . I am expecting a shipment of new astilbe any day now . . . Our radishes are

crisp and young . . . The lettuce in the cold
frame is beginning to head up . . . To-morrow
I must plant the Klondyke cosmos seeds so that
we will have blooms before frost.

Thoughts like that.

XIV

UNDER THE FIG TREE AND THE VINE

I

BUT though they lost their autocracy, books lost none of their usefulness. There was that copy of Thomas Traherne's "Centuries of Meditation." I had wanted that book just to read one sentence, and after pestering myself for three years I finally imported it. The sentence was there. It runs this way: "You will never understand the world aright until the sea itself floweth in your veins, till you are clothed with the heavens and crowned with the stars." Worth waiting three years for.

At about the same time we began to face the problem of the orchard.

Should we try to save it, or should we let it go? Most of the trees were old; some few were young, but the majority belong to the gnarled variety that looks romantic and bears little fruit. Weeks of pruning and scraping and spraying lay ahead. Innumerable wild cherry trees had also sprung up — innocuous enough to look at, but the enemy of any orchard, for the wild cherry is a generous host to worms. These would have to be cut out. Should we do it? Or should n't we? When we

examined the exchequer, it appeared that we
should n't. "Ah, well," we sighed, "it is bad for
us to be so insatiable! We must curb our garden
ambitions."

Then, in a chance moment, I opened Traherne. The words were almost a revelation. "It
is of the *nobility* of man's soul," they read, "that
he is insatiable."

There's nothing like finding a justification for
spending money you can't afford! Thank you,
Thomas Traherne! Whenever I eat of those
apples and drink of their cider, I shall remember
you. May you be in bliss to-day, may you be
clothed with the heavens and crowned with the
stars! [19]

It appeared, on studying it out, that there are
two ways of treating an orchard — as an orchard
and as a flower-garden also. The making of an
orchard that is also a flower garden may solve
the problem for those who have no woodlot and
desire to grow shade-loving and wild plants. It
may also be developed into a combination of
flower garden and orchard where the trees are
not too close together.

Two gardens that I had remembered brought
this scheme to mind. One was in the Middle
West, a flat stretch of orchard with old trees set
wide apart. Down the two middle rows an herbaceous planting had been set out, with the shade-

loving plants in immediate proximity to the trees. In the spring-time, when the borders were just showing green, the apple trees gave the heavenly pink of their blossoms; then the color changed to a lower level as tulips, iris, and peonies began the seasonal successions of bloom. The other garden was on Long Island and the two middle ranks of trees had been made into an alleyway that gave approach to a rose garden set in a clearing at the farther end of the property from the house. Up each tree was trained a climbing rose, pruned so that it never grew much higher than a man could reach and not high enough to touch the lowest branches or interfere with them. The roses did not climb on the trunk itself; they were trained up lattice that, for the greater part of the season, was invisible.

The orchard that is given to sod presents the ideal spot for naturalizing crocus, narcissus, grape hyacinth, and such other glories of spring. As they finish blossoming by the end of May, there is a good two months for the bulbs to get their season's growth before haying-time. On the other hand, should one keep an orchard very trim, with the sort of herbaceous borders mentioned above, then the bulbs can be planted in the borders and the turf will be kept cropped into grass walks, the most delightful kind of garden walks there are.

Lacking a woodlot and still desiring an orchard that was not too much a flower garden, we struck a compromise. She, who likes things wild,[20] argued for the hay crop. I, who have a passion for orderliness, argued for trim grass walks and herbaceous plantings. We compromised on keeping the hay and putting such shade-lovers as we desired here and there in out-of-the-way corners. My pet columbines have been tucked by a wall up in one corner, set out in half-shade down by the lower wall, and given a chance to prove themselves in another spot that is full sun. If you are playing with one flower to see how it behaves in various kinds of locations, then an orchard is the place to experiment in.

II

WE had hesitated touching that orchard lest there happen to us what happened to the man in Frank Stockton's story. This man, you will remember, bought a pair of andirons. When he brought them home, he found they were too big for his fireplace, so he had to enlarge the fireplace. When he had enlarged the fireplace, he realized that he had thrown his room out of scale, so he had to enlarge the room. When he had completed enlarging the room, he discovered that he had thrown the house out of proportion. In utter despair he moved out of the house.

That sort of thing often happens to people who remodel or restore old country houses and gardens. One thing necessitates another. Start to change the front step, and you'll have to change the porch, and changing the porch will require further changes in the house.

Of course, the only way to go about restoring or remodeling is to do it gradually. If it is accomplished in one season, the fun is all gone — and so is your money. What are you going to do after that? It is advisable to make the necessary interior structural changes the first year, because, after all, one does n't want to live eternally with his carpenter however nice a fellow he may be. The outside changes can then proceed gradually. But do not dream that the place will ever be finished. No, the only way to finish a place is to do as the man in Stockton's story — move out. You'll be finished long before it will.

Cleaning up the orchard meant that the orchard walls had to be re-piled. And re-piling the orchard walls meant that the brush had to be cleared away. And clearing out the brush necessitated a general grubbing of the entire orchard for the sticks and twigs that had fallen into the tall grass and gotten matted in there in such a way that they would have ruined the cutting knives and scythe at haying-time.

The same sort of thing happened to the house.

Having thrown out that bay window on my Greek temple, I accented the kitchen wing. And the kitchen wing side was very unlovely to look upon. It had, as you will recall, an uncommon skylight, in the fashion of a ship's hatch. It also had the short stub of a brick chimney surmounted by a ridiculously thin, tall stovepipe, designed to reach up and snatch passing breezes and drafts. Both of these were very bad, and we tried not to look at that side of the house. We tried to be polite about it, the way well-bred people never stare at cripples or men having a hideous disfigurement. The woodshed was also on this side of the house, bearing little or no relation to it, and was in the Italian style — the Italian style of shanty. In this mêlée of bad taste and uncouth junk, that lovely bay window looked very ill at ease.

We thought to hide it by planting a wall of tall trees — Lombardy poplars and such. This would have appeared queer, however. Passers-by and our friends would naturally have asked, "What are they ashamed of?" We despaired. Then a landscaping person came on the scene and pulled us out of the slough.

On that side of the house the land slopes perceptibly, carrying the drive up to the barn. A high stone wall has been built at this point to hold up the bank. It forms two sides of the woodshed, evidently having been excavated at the time the kitchen wing was built. One could step from this drive onto the top of the woodshed, the kitchen being ten or more feet below. We had already built a rough pergola of cedars over the kitchen walk that led to this woodshed, a pleasant bower in summer that, unfortunately, only accented the hideous shanty.

Then, as I said, along came this delightful landscaping person. She gazed upon our disfigurement and took compassion upon us. True, shrubbery was needed, badly needed, but why not take off the woodshed roof, use the rafters as a basis for a pergola, continue the pergola out where the incongruous rough cedar posts were now? The woodshed floor was of brick, and we could keep it that way. The rough stone walls could be whitewashed to conform with the house. This would make a cool, shadowed corner with a white pergola roof overhead, on which grapes could be trained.

"But what shall I do for a woodshed?" I protested. "A country house should have a woodshed."

"Nonsense!" she snorted, she who is the delight of my eyes, "Keep your wood in the cellar. That is better than harboring rats."

III

A GRAPE arbor at last!

I had wanted a grape arbor ever since Prohibition threatened to become a reality. First, I wanted to grow grapes; secondly, I wanted to be able to grow grapes because I hold to the theory that writing men write best in the localities where grapes thrive; thirdly, I wanted the sensation of sitting out, in the Biblical fashion, under my own vine and fig tree. I could not supply the fig tree, but I could at least have the vine.

Tending a grape arbor gives a man an incomparable sense of husbandry. There is that pleasant sensation of watching the leaves uncurl in spring; those moments of singing contentment when he gently lashes the tendrils with soft cord to the pergola beams; the first rapture on seeing the tiny clusters begin to swell; the careful enclosing them with bags against their pest enemies; the rich odor of the ripening fruit; the harvest tenderly picked and laid in baskets; the shriveling of the leaves at frost-time; and then the pruning of the vines so that next year the crop will be even greater. These things, I say, give a man a sense of husbandry that he does not get even from working with vegetables.

In fact, there is a joy peculiar to working with

those fruits from which wine can be made. There
is a subtle relationship between the fruit that
makes the wine and the gladness of heart that
follows on drinking it. Things in this old world
are very much closer related than we ordinarily
imagine. We usually put it down to association
of thoughts, but I believe it is more than that.

Mr. Walter Roberts, sometime editor of "Ains-
lee's Magazine," is sponsor for the theory that
men write best or congregate to write or writers
are born in those sections where the grape best
grows. The natural fermentation of the juices,
the peculiar nature of the soil that gives the vine
its abundance, the very product of the vine itself,
afford to men who create with words a subtle
inspiration. One cannot imagine Emerson roister-
ing down Boylston Street or Longfellow riding
home with his feet out the cab window; but it is
a fact that these penmen of the New England
school grew up in the same locality where flourished the Concord grape. It also is true of the
Middle-West school, which located just a little
west of the Ohio and Indiana vineyards; likewise
of the California group of writers.

With a grapevine at my door I had visions of
writing immortally. Then, too, I had thoughts
of sitting out and enjoying my leisure.

IV

In one of his essays Dion Clayton Calthrop writes: "The art of leisure lies, to me, in the power of absorbing without effort the spirit of one's surroundings; to look without speculation at the sky and the sea; to become part of a green plain; to rejoice, with a tranquil mind, in the feast of colors in a bed of flowers. To this end is a good gardener born. The man who, from a sudden love, stops in his walk to look at a field of buttercups has no idea of the spiritual advancement he has made."

To that end, also, is the good householder born; the man who, from sheer love of antiquity, can stop in the day's work to admire the patina on an old piece of furniture; who can fling wide the casements of his imagination over the valley of romance that a Japanese sword-guard shows him; who can halt midway in the rush of making money to appreciate the rare colors and fine contour of a Chinese vase. That man is gathering the fruits of leisure. He is richer every time he permits himself to enjoy these things.

I often wonder, when I see people spending money on their homes and their gardens, how much richer they actually are for this spending. Does the speed of our modern American life permit them to enjoy beautiful things? Are they spending from the sheer joy of spending or because they desire to make their homes more beautiful or more complete? And I ask myself, Have we lost the art of leisure?

We can only reap those fruits of a full life after the seed of appreciation has been given time to blossom, the bud to set and swell to fruit. We can't leap up to it in a moment. We can't buy it with money. It is a very personal acquisition requiring time and infinite patience.

It has often been said that great art flourishes only when there is an aristocracy to enjoy it, only when there is a great body of laborers to do the work for others and afford them time to appreciate beauty. The tendency of our times is to abolish these leisure classes. Our alleged aristocracy of to-day are bewailing the fact that leisure is a lost art. Perhaps their type of leisure is, and good riddance to it! They bought their leisure. In these times a man must make it.

The first step toward acquiring leisure is to decide definitely what things in life a man considers worth while. If he chooses a few simple things and those good, he will enjoy them in exactly the same measure as he labors to acquire them. But he can't have everything. He must make the choice, and having made it must stick to it as a principle in living.

This garden border that he plants, this orchard

he sets out, this Oriental rug, this vase, this
painted chest, become part of him as he becomes
part of them. He makes the choice to have them,
he labors to acquire them, and in the laboring are
sown the seeds of appreciation.

Leisure, then, is not a state in which a man sits
back and folds his hands to contemplate the
glories of his possession; leisure is a very active
state in which, as Calthrop says, he absorbs the
spirit of his surroundings without effort.

The second and fuller phase of leisure is the
sharing of it with some one else. No man owns a
house or a garden or a book to himself. The
fruits of leisure cannot be enjoyed alone. You
must share the feast. That 's the baffling aspect of
it. You no more acquire a thing than you have
to give part of it away! Once you gain possession
of it, it forthwith ceases being entirely yours.
You can enjoy it only when some one else enjoys
it, too. Mere pride of ownership is a contradic-
tion in terms.

This sharing is singularly purgative. It blots
out the memory of the effort we have expended
to acquire those things — the abnegations that
pulled down a bit of Heaven to our tiny plot of
soil, the sacrifices that have brought us those
flowered curtains blowing in the window.

So we come to the definition of leisure as an
active state of sharing appreciation and enjoy-

ment, a state where labor ceases its babel, where ownership lays aside its talk of mine and thine, and only loveliness is eloquent.

No, leisure is not a lost art to-day. It is a different sort of art.

XV
GARDENS THAT ARE AND ARE TO BE

I

SOME pages back I stated that I preferred to garden *coram populo*. I cannot hold with the English theory of enclosing all gardens with walls, because, just as a man may not possess leisure to himself, or live a life to himself, so he cannot make a garden to himself.

Try to keep a garden beautiful to yourself alone and see what happens — the neighbor, hurrying by to catch his train of mornings, will stop to snatch a glint of joy from the iris purpling by your doorstep. The motorist will throw on brakes and back downhill just to see those Oriental poppies massed against the wall.

Nature is always on the side of the public. Build your wall never so high but her winds will carry the seeds of that choice variety you reserved for yourself to a dozen different dooryards and open fields, where they will blossom next season. Plant your hedgerow never so thick but a vine will stretch forth a friendly finger through it. Lock the gate never so tight but the zephyrs will waft odors of rose and hyacinth and mignonette to every passer-by.

It follows, then, that a garden is a public service and having one a public duty. It is a man's contribution to the community. It is not enough that law and order be preserved in our communities. Only the policeman with his truncheon would stand between us and chaos if law and order were all we desired. No, it is the mark of an upward-looking civilization that men make beautiful gardens, that the joy of the tulip and the flowering shrub be shared with other men.

II

THIS is the philosophy behind the making of the gardens on our seven acres more or less. This was the sort of sentiment we returned to those who suggested our walling in the front lawn with tall shrubs and piling shrubbery along the back of the long herbaceous border. Herbaceous borders should have a background; that is true; but if you cut off your view to the distant hills, if you hide that border's beauty from those coming up your own hill, then you are very much mistaken in your theory of gardening.

This long border was a problem that could have been solved readily had we moved out and the landscapist moved in. But that sort of garden we had no intention of making. So we labored over maps and color schemes and catalogues and battled and argued and questioned and compromised, until, finally, there was evolved a scheme that would give us our favorite flowers in a succession of bloom.

We had started by making the backbone of this border a middle row of German iris and peonies, with some of the iris coming well to the front to give the occasional accent of unusual height. English daisies, raised in the upper seed-bed behind the vegetable garden, made an irregular front line, broken here and there with pansies and violas and later-blooming low things, such as sweet alyssum. In one corner, where a fir gave background, was placed a shoal of white phlox, with a mass of delphinium Rev. E. Lascelles beside it. This combination was repeated at the farther end and again in the middle. Foxglove, Canterbury bells, and hollyhocks gave height along the back, with cosmos moved in in late spring from the annual garden. Massed here and there went groups of Japanese iris and some Siberian iris "Purple King." Helinium gave us a fall bronze. Bee-balm, furnished a deep red in midsummer. Geums in little groups gave brilliant spots of color. I even tempted the ire of garden friends by putting in, in midsummer, little drifts of marigolds, lemon and gold, and white and blue asters to follow along before the Michaelmas daisies. Some few groups of bronze and yellow hardy chrysanthemums further enliven the autumn.

Below the wall, at the top edge of the meadow, and forming a lower tier of this border, is set a long line of tall cosmos and the ubiquitous golden glow, making a tidal wave of color and delicate greenery from July on, punctuated with the significant yellow of the golden glow, the white of early cosmos and, later, the red, pink, and white of the ordinary fall cosmos.

Without a map, which I have no intention of drawing, the scheme of planting cannot be appreciated. It is very unorthodox and disorderly and apparently unkempt. But this is her garden, and she has a penchant for wildish effects. She says that a border should n't look as if it had just had a permanent wave.

III

BUT if there was a jungle effect in color and leafage in the long border, it served a definite purpose — as a contrast to what is beyond. This border runs along a stretch of lawn, and at the end a little planting of cedars develops into a formal garden — her little formal garden. Cedars were taken from Doglands, across the road, and set in their native soil, rank on rank of them, enclose a little spot with grass paths and a burst of color at the end in front of the taller cedars. Here is placed a tiny pool, simple in outline and without pretension, to mirror the stars and clouds and sky, a little jewel — now sapphire, now ruby, now garnet, now topaz — in a setting of green. Every garden should have some form of water, even if it is only a tub sunk in the sod and big enough to hold a water-lily. The garden with running water — a brook, a waterfall — ah, what possibilities! For of the music in the garden none is more lovely than the *pizzicato* of dripping water or the *rondo* of a babbling stream.

The rear cedar wall of this little formal garden is in line with our projected rose garden. Perhaps it is bad taste to repeat one's dreams, to speak of that which the lean purse may never permit one to attain. So far in developing these few acres we have gone on the very bad economic principle of doing what we could not afford and then working day and night to afford it. That is doubtless the way the rose garden will come; I see no other way.

This, if you please, will have a wall, for the simple reason that the slope which is there now faces north, the slope now naturalized to a multitude of narcissus. At the orchard end it will be higher than my head, and in that sheltered position espalier fruit can be trained on the west and north walls. The east wall need not be so high, as it leads off the *tapis vert* behind my study porch. This will be broken by low, broad steps giving gradual approach to the level of the rose garden.

On the north side steep stone steps will lead
down to the level of the little formal garden; on
the south side a gate will open on the kitchen
garden. There will be big work in leveling down
that slope and a vast expenditure for manure
and lime and Scotch soot, but there is no use
starting a rose garden unless you start it right.
Like a wife, a rose garden is a distinct luxury,
and one should not enter upon either of them
lightly or without first counting the cost. Not
that lovely roses cannot be grown and are grown
without a great outlay of money. Better have a
few roses in a border than no roses at all.

Or you may look at the rose habit this way —
start with a few and learn the simple requirements in handling those few. The beginner stands
in terror of the various rose pests and sprays
and kinds of mulch and stimulating plant foods
that various writers and seedsmen recommend.
Like learning German irregular verbs or, what is
worse, Russian verbs, every case seems to differ,
every little curl of leaf and spot on petal calls
for a new kind of spray. It will greatly simplify
matters when the beginning gardener finds that
most of these sprays can be reduced to one, and
that common sense, not deep garden intellectu-
ality, lies behind the various treatments suggested for roses. I feel that this pest and spray
side of rose-growing has been exaggerated, and

that many people who would otherwise pay a great deal of attention to roses have been scared off.

IV

WHILE the rose garden was held in abeyance, the autumn border went ahead. A broad strip sprawling up the hill alongside the road to the barn and the kitchen garden was turned over for the frosts and snow to sweeten. I watched that plot lovingly through two blizzards and innumerable zero days. For there remained indelibly in my mind a vision I had seen at the Royal Horticultural Society's fall exhibition at Vincent Square the year before — a vision of Michaelmas daisies and hardy chrysanthemums, the like of which I never knew could be grown. There was also imprinted on that gray matter the picture of many beds of tritoma flaming that fall at Kew. I had made a solemn promise before I left London that somewhere in those seven acres more or less would be builded an autumn border where Michaelmas daisies and the hardy pompoms and a range of knipfolia would flourish into Indian summer.

Because they grow wild in our New York and New England meadows we are apt to neglect the possibilities of the starwort asters — the Michaelmas daisies. English nurserymen have developed them with remarkable success, great

blossoms great flurries of clustered blooms that
are so beautiful to look upon that you eat your
heart out with envy for them. The hardy chrysanthemums, of course, we do grow in abundance,
and we need not blush for those shown at our fall
flower exhibitions.

The knipfolia, on the other hand, is passing
under a cloud just at present. We know them,
our landscape architects say, "Oh, yes," when
you mention them, and our nurserymen nod
knowingly. But they all mention how undeco-
rative the foliage looks, and that seems to be
about all there is to it. Trying to be enthusiastic
about tritomas just now is like mentioning to a
family of the socially elect the wayward small
brother who got infatuated with a waitress and
married her. They won't say anything against
him, but you can gather, from the tone of voice,
that they won't say much for him.

The case against tritomas isn't so much the
foliage as it is the psychology of their color. We
may talk about a heavenly blue delphinium or the
fierce red of salvia or the fragile flames of the
poppies, and yet it cannot be said that American
gardeners are entirely converted to the use of
strong color. People still refer to "pastel shades"
in the garden. Now, the tritoma is anything but
a pastel shade, although many varieties have a
subtle blending of red, yellow, and green tones in

them. Taken *en masse*, they are bold, strong color. They do not blend gently, they are direct and imposing and vital. Showy? Yes. But we need such showy points for accents in our gardens. We may think them crude and unlovely, but I'm reminded of the fact that the brilliant, contrasting colors one finds in the parks of Paris have a beauty that is remembered when all the pussyfoot pastel blending in other gardens is forgotten. We need some of that direct color in our American gardens, and tritomas will give it.

So this border was made broad and deep, to accommodate perennials that would afford color from midsummer on into the late fall. Poppies are planted at intervals for a succession of bloom — Shirleys and some white annuals saved from a garden in Surrey and some that Luther Burbank has created. Gypsophila flore pleno marks the transition from color to color. Verbena spreads here and there along the front. Little clumps of annual chrysanthemums add to the midsummer glory. Snapdragons, tawny red and golden brown and yellow, range down the middle of the bed — these also from seeds saved in that Surrey garden. And behind them, astilbe, delphinium, tritomas, statice, Michaelmas daisies, and many dahlias, with lower clumps of the hardy mums in red, claret, white, yellow, and bronze.

Of autumn days I like to climb the hill to my

vegetable garden and rest there a moment looking
back on this display. It is the last challenge of
the year — but what a challenge! What a gorgeous finale, this autumn border!

V

THE garden shows three degrees of vigor. First,
the resurgent vigor of spring, lusty up-thrust of
myriad blades and breathless rush to break into
flower. Next, the full tide of summer, the robust
growing. Then the mellow days of autumn.
After that the waning.

Each has its own rare colors and revelations of
beauty. It is difficult to say which season gives
the most delight. The gardener, though, who has
followed the cycle of work (and only he who does
the work really appreciates it) finds the autumn
garden full of fascinating and subtle moods.

September comes to us as a woman blessed with
a great inheritance, whose lines have fallen in fair
places. She has the flash and flame of leaves that
begin to turn, she is colorful with blossoms, and
she wears a scarf of blue mist around her shoul-
ders. But think of all the glories that have been
handed down to her from August!

These three months — August, September,
and October — remind me of three sisters endowed with diminishing amounts of this world's
goods. Late August possesses an abundance —

innumerable asters, the white of sneezewort, the mallows, various sunflowers and golden glow, the flaming of tritoma and the diversity of early chrysanthemums. Many of these she passes on to September, and what September has left she hands on down for October to deck herself in during her final festive days of Indian summer. Then frosts whiten the fields before the approach of November. Poor thing, there's naught left November save some gaudy berries — the last bits of old family jewelry that even the poorest are too proud to part with.

It is this gradual ebbing of the garden's vigor that makes so many people look upon autumn as a season of regrets. The old Chinese poet, Lu Yun, has expressed the feeling perfectly in a beautiful line: "At the fall of the year there is autumn in my heart."

Once frost robs the garden of color, once the rich silhouette of tall flower clumps and bushes and leafy trees is reduced to rattling skeletons, then comes autumn in the heart. And yet, this is strange, for the autumn months are among the busiest in the garden year.

Think of all there is to do in autumn — the divisions and transplanting, the setting of bulbs, the mulching and enriching of the beds, the harvesting of dahlia roots and gladiolus bulbs, the covering of perennials, the bringing of plants indoors to winter over in that sunny bay window, the tucking of others away in the cold frame.

Many people make the mistake of thinking that autumn marks the end of the garden year. Autumn is only the garden's ultimate perfection, and the ultimate perfection of a thing, as the philosopher has said, is that it is the beginning of something new.

Even in the chill north wind there is the promise of spring balminess. The withered stalk holds a hint of greater abundance next season. In this autumn's smashed and scraggly lily clump is hidden the beginning of a larger clump next year. On every hand is this promise of something new and something better. In the irreparable past of autumn lurks the available future of another garden year.

Next Year is the constant Life-to-Come of gardeners. The mistakes of this year will be rectified then. The undesirable colors will be rooted out of that perennial border. The iris that never did do well where it is will be given another change in another environment. Those special strains of snapdragons and sweet peas you've been longing to try will find a place in next year's garden.

Next Year! Next Year!

The autumn mood of the garden-lover is quickened by this beginning of something new; it is strong with a promise of fulfillment.

XVI

ON ATTAINING DOMESTIC WISDOM

I

ONE day I was emboldened to ask her a question. I waited until she was seated in her *chaise longue* and the fire was blazing merrily and the room had warmed up. It was a moment for confidences.

"Tell me, Light of My Eyes," I asked, "why did you ever call this the morning room? Why not the parlor?"

She was silent for a moment, and then she replied, in the manner of Scheherazade, "It hath reached me, O auspicious King, that when the parlor was first created, it was designed as a place to talk in. *Parler*, as they say in France. And it was so for many years. Then a great darkness fell upon the land and men took to singing Gospel Hymns and women worried over the pomps and vanities of this wicked world and all the sinful lusts of the flesh. They also dressed accordingly. The art of conversation died, but the parlor remained.

"You can remember that parlor, Carissimo. Your great-aunt, who used to talk about the death-beds of the Episcopal bishops, had one. Its blinds were drawn and the air was musty and chill. The carpet was vivid red with cabbage roses tied in garlands of pale-blue ribbon. A suite of horsehair furniture ranged stiffly against the walls. It held pillows of varicolored and tufted silks. In the corner stood the whatnot with the mementoes of trips to the World's Fair and Altoona that your great-aunt took. Your grandfather and grandmother were hung above the bricked-up fireplace — kindly old souls done in crayon and with a fine disregard for perspective. In the center of the room stood a marble-topped table with a red plush cover on it, and on that the Bible. A hassock was on each side of the empty hearth. The curtains were lace — immaculate lace and very stiff. Because of the memory of that room, Carissimo, and the memories I have of many another like it, I would rather not have this home than be obliged to call this room a parlor."

I remained silent, for her words reminded me bitterly of my youth. That parlor of which she spoke was rarely opened, except to be cleaned, or when, on two sad occasions, relatives were laid in their coffins. Once a bishop came to call, I remember, and the parlor was opened then and we had tea. I was permitted to come in and shake hands with him. He had a long beard and was very ancient, and I was mortally afraid lest he would ask me to recite "My Duty to My Neighbor."

Between us that night we agreed that the parlor was an excrescence on the American home, and those who love life and laughter and sunlight have done well to fling wide the windows and doors, throw away the horsehair furniture, the crayon portraits, and the mementoes from Altoona, open up the fireplace and make that room possible to live in.

A parlor was a rank affectation in the day when no one conversed brilliantly. Life in the Gospel Hymn Era really centered around the red-cotton covered table in the kitchen and the organ in the dining-room. Since we've given up Gospel Hymns and stiff chairs and gone in for Debussy, jazz, and *chaises longues*, we require a room in which all these moods may be exercised twenty-four hours out of the day.

It may be that we pack more into our twenty-four hours than our forefathers did, we may sleep less, eat less and live more intensely. For us life is constantly beginning to-morrow, and our houses show it. We have a reverent affection for the past and for the way things were done in those days, but we will not permit the past to dominate our lives. Fashions change in architecture and furnishing just as they do in clothes. The eternal flux of life demands that we be willing to lay aside the old and take on the new when new life and new manners demand. Each room in the house must be a background for some phase of our changing, varying life. It must be an environment that we vitalize the moment we step into it. No room has a right to exist save it exist for people to live in it every day or any day.

There is no place in the modern home for rooms that are not used, just as there is no place in the modern room for furniture that does not serve to increase the comfort and convenience of the body or quicken the pulse at the sight of good line and harmonious color. When any room ceases to serve that end, it will pass, even as the parlor has passed, out of existence.

On my way upstairs that night, as I was retiring to my cot in Orphant Annie's Room, content that I had attained more wisdom, a question came suddenly to me. I leaned over the banister to ask it.

"But why did you call it a morning room?"

"Because every one else in town calls theirs a living-room," she replied.

I thought that a very sensible answer.

II

I was also emboldened, during this winter, to speculate on the mystery of collecting, which I mentioned a few chapters back. Being married to a collector of old lights, being the son of a stamp collector, the brother-in-law of a lace collector, the nephew of a book collector, and the cousin by marriage to a collector of silver snuff-boxes, I thought that I ought to learn, by mere contact, why it is that people collect.

The collector of old books, who was a parson, a master of fourteen tongues and a saint besides, vouchsafed to me the simple truth that only three things build walls around men and make them unapproachable—age, wealth, and position. But, he added, if they are collectors, none of these has the slightest effect. These distinctions dissolve in the presence of common interest that the habit of collecting engenders. The one universal element in all collectors would seem to be a form of whimsicality, of unaccountable affections and attractions. Romance flames high in him and his bump of reverence is abnormally developed.

Romance and reverence as a collector feels them are mostly of the past tense. To him an old chair is more than something to sit on. It is a chair that belonged to So-and-So, who lived at such and such a time, or it was the work of this master hand, or in the style of that designer. For these things he has reverence. He is also quickened by the romantic past of the object and by his own romance in acquiring it. His possession of it is the last item in a long pedigree that includes the maker, the men and women who have owned it from time to time, the house it has graced, the worthy folk who have admired it, the twists and turns of fortune that made it pass from hand to hand until good luck made it his.

Apart from the market valuation of his collected objects, the collector has a standard of values that is purely personal — the valuation his enthusiasm places upon it. Anything is at a premium to him so long as he wants it.

Naturally not all collectors go in for antiques; the curiosity and the novelty are quite as collectible, and the man who seeks them is as genuine a collector as the millionaire whose hobby costs him fortunes. As there are different grades of men, so there are different grades of collectors. One may go in for Chinese ceramics, another for Rembrandts, a third for valentines, and a fourth for old painted tin trays. In all of them burns the same ardor of romance and reverence. They are brothers under their hides.

To a genuine collector the mere act of possession in no wise compares with the adventure of acquiring. For when a man has assembled a fairly good collection of any one object, he forthwith loses interest in it and begins another. It is complete when it is the beginning of something new.

Collections change hands, it seems, on the average of every ten or fifteen years. It takes about

that time to assemble a good collection. Interest
is then diverted to something else, and the collection put on the market and scattered. Thus
the romance is perpetuated for other collectors.
So there is nothing selfish about collection; human interest has a saturation point that prevents
selfishness.

I was glad to be able to think this out, because
I was trying to link up the relation between love
of home and love of collecting. I have never met
a radical radical — the bomb-free-love-and-un-
washed kind — who cares the slightest about collecting. It seems to be the virtue of those who
have a home, who love their home, and who ex-
pend their greatest energies on making that home
more comfortable and convenient and beautiful
to look upon.[31]

III

THIS desire of mine to acquire domestic wisdom
may appear a little too ingenuous to be true. I
assure you it was very real and very true. In the
course of my somewhat limited experience with
life I have found that a man must think through
every situation in which he finds himself. The
mere acceptance of the commonplace things in a
home is not enough; before he can find his real
strength he must master the philosophy of the
commonplace. I found myself with an old house

to remodel and an old garden to rejuvenate. It was not enough for me to learn that some plants are started in hotbeds and some where they are to grow; I wanted to learn the idea that underlay it all. I wanted to feel gardening besides practicing it. So also with the house. Coming from a New York apartment where space was limited and freedom reduced to its ultimate minimum, I found myself peculiarly bewildered by the sense of release that an upstairs and a down give. I was not accustomed to that assurance of respectability which owning property gave me. These new sensations only served to convince me that, though I might learn how to run a furnace and be a handy man around the garden, that home would be wasted on me until I thought it through and had mastered the philosophy of it.

Having mastered it, I could either accept or reject — accept it and be contented, or reject it and continue suffering from what seemed my incurable malady, the loose foot.

XVII

CURING THE LOOSE FOOT

I

Some men are born domesticated; some have civilization married into them; others can never be tamed. A wife, a job, a family, responsibilities, all are fretful obligations, not because they are obligations, but because they stake a man to one spot. Thousands of men live like the cow staked in a pasture, only able to nibble and rove the length of his chain!

We were both born with a loose foot and we marveled that we had stayed in one spot as long as we had. There was that villa up in the hills outside of Florence and a tiny apartment on the Rue du Bac in the midst of the Quartier; there was that stretch of steppe land in Siberia, glorious in spring-time, and that pungent odor of the East; there was a river in Cochin-China still to be explored and a summer to be passed in the Vale of Cashmir; there was a winter in Ceylon and a season in Java; there was a little hotel in Petit Angelis and a cottage in Surrey. For years these promises lay wrapped up in the backs of our minds, like fine laces that one puts carefully away and then brings forth years later for glorious enrichment. When we undertook that Greek temple on a Connecticut hilltop, it was almost an act of disloyalty to ourselves; every penny that went into it put the fulfillment of our promises farther and farther from us.

We were not content. We never shall be content. Speak a word and the fire of far places flames within us. Some day! Some day! And then the tether jerks us back to reality.

"If you can't realize your ideal," Emerson says, "idealize your real." So we set about to do it, to find in the things and the persons about us some panacea, some cure for the loose foot.

Mélaine, our *bonne*, understands not a word of English. She runs us and the house in the patois of Ariège, so that French and Italian do equally well with her. I type out the menus and orders for the week in a culinary French full of the romantic names of eminent Gallic *gourmets*. She also superintends my labors in the vegetable garden. Any one coming suddenly upon us might think that another war had broken out — she shouting at the top of her lungs at me in French, I answering back equally vociferously in English. The subject? How corn should be planted. We argue and make signs and look it up in French and American seed catalogues. Finally we compromise — one row is planted *à la Français*, the next *à la Américain*.

Once I started to introduce an English lad to help out in the garden, but the Gallic cook flew into a rage, and he had to be dismissed. In fact, the Gallic cook is a true patriot. The Austrian painter who came up from New York to finish the panels in the hall almost had to go without his supper on patriotic grounds. He finally got it by claiming that he was a Czecho-Slovak. The touch-and-go feeling between France and England is constantly being reflected in our household, and English friends who visit us have to be explained away as Canadians. On the other hand, when, in an unguarded moment, I brought home some old copies of "La Vie Parisienne," she scolded me for being a bad boy and flourished before my eyes a silver chainful of medals that she fished from her blouse — the four and twenty medals for the four and twenty pilgrimages she made for France and her desperately wounded *mari* during the war.[22]

We have put down Mélaine against that apartment in the Rue du Bac. As against the East we put down those Japanese panels in the hall — the ones with the carmine chrysanthemums on each side the hall mirror. As against that season in Java must stand the hanging above the chimney shelf in my study, a piece of batik in the Javanese manner. As against the rest of the world that lures us, the garden.

All gardens to-day are more or less international. The man with a well-planted garden literally has the world at his feet. In the length of his pathside border he touches the farther reaches of the five continents and the innumerable isles. The hollyhock brings a message from China, the anemone speaks of Japan. The long-spurred columbine represents the Rockies and the vulgaris types Siberia. Transylvania has given us the bellflower and Armenia the star thistle. The Peruvian lily comes up the continent to us and the day-lily travels from the far-off Amur Valley. Hot Asia Minor is represented by one kind of poppy and the Arctic regions by another. The dahlia reminds us that Mexico is only next door, the tulip speaks for cheese and Holland, the geranium for Africa. He travels far who has a garden. It will not, to be sure, answer entirely for the East or the smell of Paris or the constant view of the Himalayas from a Cashmir Valley boathouse, but it will serve to make the years pass more contentedly.

Look upon this bold row of cabbages heading up proudly, and the vision of that yet-to-be-explored river in Cochin-China fades into nothingness . . . An August evening; the moon is upon her back, and you feel the dampness of coming rain. The air grows rich with the scent of night stocks and verbena and mignonette.

Somehow, that heavy, pungent, unwashed odor of
a Chinese treaty port loses its tang in your nostrils.

The loose foot is a curse or a blessing according
to the measure of the things a man brings back
from the foreign parts in which he has roamed.
These day-lilies clustered by my study door are
more lovely than ever to me, because I can recall
the drifts of them I saw once in sheltered dells
along the Amur in Upper Manchuria. They are
lovely, too, because of the bank of them, not a
hundred yards from my white meadow gate,
growing wild along the roadside. I shall perhaps
never go back to those hidden little valleys of the
Amur, but I have brought here, to this Connecticut hilltop, the memory of their beauty. With
this much I must be satisfied.

II

Even in the face of such poignant experiences
I would not say that every man should garden.
Gardening does not come naturally to every man:
we should not expect it of him, any more than
expecting all men to be great lovers and all
women mothers of children and good cooks.

Some people make a garden because it is a
fashionable thing to do. They have themselves
photographed for society magazines and Sunday
supplements, in their gardens (made by their
hosts of gardeners), wearing smart clothes and all

the jeweled panoply of Dives.   I have a notion
that when such pictures are taken the little birds
in the tree-tops have a difficult time to prevent
themselves from bursting with laughter.   And
yet I know that the interest of society women in
gardening has a salutary effect.   They are the
bellwether sheep of a flock of suburban wives who,
until they heard that Mrs. Chomley-Chomley
works in her garden, had a vague notion that
getting one's hands dirty with soil was among the
things that were n't done.

Other people take gardening the way they
would take a narcotic (the way some men take
work) — to make themselves forget the bitter
realities of life.   This is futile because, to maintain
the stimulus for oblivion they must increase the
dose, and they eventually reach the point where
they are not capable of increasing it.

Still others make gardens because it is part of a
full life.   To live happily they must invest their
hours and aspirations in the activities of another
world.   And they draw the interest of delight and
refreshment according to the measure of their
investment.   These are usually quaint folk, other-
worldly in their manner, but capable of compre-
hending the idiosyncrasies of Nature as she dis-
plays them in tree and bush and passing season,
across the skyline and in the infinite zenith.
These, moreover, are the successful gardeners.

III

Some people are referred to as "born gardeners." They are n't necessarily scientific or intellectual (quite the opposite in most cases), but they seem to have a knack for making plants grow. Others may spend money freely for fine tools and chemicals and especially selected seeds; whereas some poor little old woman in a back street, who can't afford all these luxuries, makes her wilderness blossom like the rose.

What is the answer?

To have beautiful roses in your garden, Dean Hole once wrote, you must first have them in your heart. That's the reason.

The little old woman, like as not, raises her flowers the same way she raises her babies. She does it herself. It is part of the day's work, this making her dooryard beautiful. Upon her own energies depends the success of that garden. She does n't lay off because the sun is hot, and she has n't any gardener to hand the tools over to when the work grows irksome. She does n't garden because it is the fashion, but because flowers are pretty things to have about the place and because her man and her children enjoy fresh vegetables. They are a vital part of her everyday life.

And when you get to know that little old woman (which may not be so easy), you will find her to have some amazing habits. Start her on the subject of flowers and vegetables and she 'll talk about them familiarly, poetically, like the lover in the Song of Solomon, with quaint observations that open doors to vast worlds of deep understanding. And midway in her conversation she will stop and look up lovingly at some fluffy cloud drifting across the sky or listen to the call of a bird or let her eyes rest understandingly on a hill far away where the tawny checkerboard fields spill over the horizon. Caught in the upward encircling of Nature she is gazing upon another world.

" The good God," as some Frenchman said, has seen to it that most of gardening is done on the knees. From the knees one is best uplifted — going easily from cabbages to clouds, from this nadir of cutworms to that zenith of cherubim.

Having seen how crowded the streets of the sky are, having been pleasantly bewildered by the puissance of it all, she turns again to the flowers at her feet — and they are lovelier for that contrast, delphinium are bluer for that sky, and phlox whiter for the clouds, and the brown earth more golden for those tawny fields on the hilltop over there.

IV

THERE are many fair things to look upon in this old world — the smile that greets your home-

coming of nights, the mist wraiths about tall
buildings in the dusk, the pure colors of a medi-
æval lacquer — and one of these very fair is a
garden.

In the spring there is the strangely fragile lush
grass and the golden loveliness of mornings that
make you feel as though you are in at the beginning of a new Creation. In summer come the si-
esta hours — the baked noontide heat when va-
pors float over the earth like levitation and the
poppy bows her head in the garden close until the
cool rains of evening raise it again. Dusks are
ours — quiet, mauve summer dusks when we sit
quietly watching the countryside darken into
night, seeing the fireflies hang their lanterns on
stalk and branch. Then come the crisp days of
autumn when tree and bush are flame and Nature
is mightily consumed on her pyre, like some
old Indian princess majestically sorrowful in her
suttee.

These things, I say, are fair to look upon, and a
man is a better man for having seen them. But if
he knows not the touch of earth, he will never see
them; if he raises not his eyes, he will be blinded
to their glory.

For a garden is more than stem and blossom
and brown earth. It is infinitely greater than anything you can create with diligent labor. In the
huge mosaic of the countryside your garden may

be only a small piece, but it shares the glory and the wonder of everything about it. To see, to understand these is the ultimate compensation of gardening. It will make a man rejoice in being tied to one spot.

v

SCARCELY a man living but has his apartment on the Rue du Bac; scarcely a woman but has her villa on a hillside beyond Florence. This desire to be somewhere else, this thirst for drinking "strange frenzy from the wind," is part and parcel of human nature. It annoys, pesters, lures, haunts, and tempts. You can compromise with it, but that ghost is not easily laid. The only way to master it is to get irrevocably in debt through a country house. In other words, do as the cow — be staked to one spot by a short chain.

Getting ourselves acclimated to the realities of this Connecticut hilltop constituted as distinct and strenuous a struggle as any two people could go through and come out still married. We had not chosen the line of least resistance in saddling ourselves with that place. After the first novelty of it wore off, we had to buckle down to the real work of being orientated from city existence to country living.

It is quite easy to visualize one's self — as every incipient member of the landed gentry

does — in the Lord of the Manor rôle, the portly
gentleman who stalks about his tiny estate giving
orders, overseeing the live stock and inspecting
the berry patch. It is very simple for a woman to
picture herself as the Lady of the Manor — a slim
figure in organdie and a big hat among her roses.
It is quite another matter to bridge over that
gulf between the first pair of sporty rural knickerbockers and the crude and unlovely pair of khaki
pants, between the breakfast-in-bed wife and the
servantless slave of an oil stove. And yet the
most direct way to get down to country living is
to buy the khaki pants and the oil stove first.
The way to rid one's self of those far-off white
walls of Babylon is to pitch in and do one's own
work.

After the first season, after the first corn is
plucked, the first poppies cut, the first apples
harvested — ah, then, the open road and the
South Sea isles begin to lose some of their terrors.
You can then look a steamship catalogue in the
face without a tremor. You can turn the picture
of Paris to the wall without regret. The horse-
chestnuts on the Champs Élysées may go on
blossoming forever; you are contented with your
elms.

XVIII
THE LAST CHAPTER — WHICH IS ON HEAVEN

I

A FRIEND climbed our hill one day — the same friend for whom we had opened that lovely bottle of "Vat 41," the same who had told us that our blessed hilltop could be purchased. He wanted to speak to me, and from the long expression on his face I gathered that he wanted to speak to me alone. Perhaps I had violated some regulation of the town or my dog had killed a chicken. I took him into the study, closed the door, pushed an easy-chair toward him, and produced the hard-cider jug.

"It's on going to church," he began.

"Has any one been doing it?" I asked, filling his glass.

"Most every one but you." Then he waited an impressive period, set down his glass, and gestured as if he were about to sell me something. "I have a theory that a man who owns property in a town should go to a church in that town."

"Like joining the country club," I suggested.

"Precisely."

He would have said more had I not filled his

glass again. It was clear that we had violated a
regulation. Church-going was evidently "done"
in that neighborhood. I recalled that a certain
society woman, not many days before, had confided to me the salient fact that it was not con-
sidered good taste for the guests of a country-
house party to arise on Sundays before eleven.
We thought we were in the mode; evidently we
were not.

The following Sunday we declared a morato-
rium on gardening and prepared for church. She
put on her new dress — the pink one with the
gillyflowers growing up the skirt — and the big
pink floppy hat, and I arrayed myself in a stiff
collar and the double-breasted blue serge of which
I am so proud because of my recently acquired
slimness. Mélaine, who was to worship according
to the Roman rite, affixed about her neck the four
and twenty medals of the four and twenty pilgrimages, saw to it that her rosary and a quarter
were in her purse, and off we went.

I am glad we went. Not that I came out any
different a man than I went in, but because I
got such a good view of Heaven.

The sermon was very dull — a polemic on
dogma. I especially detest polemics on dogma,
for I hold that no man to-day is converted by
syllogisms. I tried to amuse myself by reading
the Thirty-Nine Articles in the back of the Prayer

Book and by calculating that the marriage service
consumed only seven minutes. Finally, having
come to the end of my distractions, I turned in
desperation to a pious book that some previous
occupant had left in the pew. It contained a
translation of St. Bernard's "Hora Novissima"
— "O Sweet and Blessed Country." After that
I did n't care how long the preacher argued. My
mind was filled with pleasant — albeit unseemly
— thoughts.

Unless I am mistaken, this St. Bernard person
has been lying on his sacred tummie on the floor
of Heaven and peeking down upon our place
through a star hole. In fact, it was rather dis-
couraging, after having written several thousand
words on that place, to find that a twelfth-cen-
tury monk had done it all before me, and done it
infinitely better.

It gave me a peculiar sort of joy to read —

> The palace that reëchoes
> With festive song and mirth . . .

I remembered that I had intended writing of
my own efforts at minstrelsy, especially the songs
I sing in my bath. Before this time I had hoped
to explain the difference between singing in a
city bathroom and singing in a country, the
former being quite impossible, the latter quite a
joy. I wanted to explain why my bathing reper-

toire contained such tunes as "Christian, dost
thou see them?" — the perfect hymn for the
basso profundo which most men sing in their
baths; "The Lover's Curse" — a plaintive Irish
tune that goes well with soaping; and "When
Dull Care" — an old English song that I always
"do" whilst the water runs.

This thought, of course, took me completely
out of church. I went on with my St. Bernard
meditation —

> And martyrdom hath roses
> Upon that heavenly ground,
> And white and virgin lilies
> For virgin souls abound.

This struck me as quite a pretty sentiment. I
promised myself to remember it the next time I
was spraying aphids off the Aaron Wards.

> The pastures of the blessed
> Are decked in glorious sheen

was peculiarly apt, because, just at this time, our
meadow below the house was decked in a really
glorious sheen of daisies and buttercups and the
French battle-field poppies that I had naturalized
there.

> And through the sacred lilies
> And flowers on every side
> The happy, dear-bought people
> Go wandering far and wide.

That touched me almost to tears. I very nearly repented having said that I wanted to drink my coffee in the lily-bed like the lover in Solomon's Song. The vision of this Bernardian Heaven was very real and very intense. There was no doubt of it — his feet had known our Connecticut acreage. Did he not describe the fruit trees the Scandinavian had pruned and the berry bushes that I had bought only that year from Scheepers and Lovett of Little Silver?

> O princely bowers! O land of flowers!
> O realm and home of life!

I was so exalted that I almost forgot to drop my money into the contribution plate.

II

EVERY man, of course, has a right to his own conception of Heaven. During the course of my limited and uneventful years I have had occasion to set down in my journal no less than twenty-seven different conceptions of that place. At another time and in another book I may write of them — the Heaven of the Cooks, to which go all men and women who have concocted viands to tickle the palate of hungry men; and the Heaven of Mediocrity, which is called Brooklyn; and the especial Heaven outside the gates prepared for lovers of dogs; and the Paradise of those who have composed lovely tunes, where the fiddle-strings never snap and the pianos never get out of tune. These things I will surely write, even if a publisher refuses to bring them out. Let be! Let be!

There is only space to talk on the Heaven of those who, having dwelt a long space in cities, relinquish the convenient restaurant, the merry club, the handy delicatessen, and all the blessings of cities, for solitary hilltops where they make them a home and build a garden.

The kitchen in that home will have rows of burnished pots that keep themselves clean, and white-curtained, wide casements that look out over star-strewn meadows. There you will find Brother Lawrence, superintending the cooking, assisted by the moon-faced frau from Pottstown, Pennsylvania, who first made scrapple (a heavenly breakfast dish), and the hatchet-faced but competent Puritan who baked the initial Boston bean and slid the first codfish ball into its baptismal fat. There, on the kitchen stoop, beneath the shadow of the skylight that looks like a ship's hatch, the children shall linger waiting for candy pots to lick. And old Noah will come in for his nips of cooking sherry, come in rubbing his rheumaticky hands and muttering, "Kinda cold this mornin'!"

To the eastward, set like a trap to catch the sunrise, will be a wide terrace with the blue sky for roof, and lanterns stolen from many churches giving it light, and easy-chairs from the heathen Chinee and the merry Italian rubbing elbows side by side. There also will be books to read — all the books that we never found time even to open — and whilst we eat, we shall make merry over Boswell's "Life of Johnson" and Blackstone's "Commentaries on Common Law."

The house will have a morning room, and in it will linger, in a négligée soft as dusk, a most lovely lady with eyes like the stars and a voice that is as the music of many waters. Behind it will be a study with countless books, shelf on shelf of them, that could never be afforded in this life, and he who comes in there will always have brains enough to understand what the books are about.

Upstairs there will be a Blue Room and a Yellow Room and an Apricot Room, and a room for Orphant Annie, with a cot that has no lumps and a sea-chest with a lid that closes softly. There will be no bureau in it. Nor in the cellar will there be rats.

St. Francis will tend the flowers and for helpers he will have sinners to water the plants with their tears. Nebuchadnezzar will tend to the lawn, because of his early fondness for grass, and Ruth can crop the wheat. The rose there will know no aphid nor the hollyhock rust, and the cabbage shall head into perfection, innocent of the cut-worm. Nor killing frosts, nor torrential rains, nor destructive winds shall this garden know, nor the soil crusted with baking heat. There the sun shall smile down gently and the columbines shall grow lustily like weeds.

In fact, that mansion will be not unlike this Greek temple with a bay window, those gardens not unlike these seven acres, more or less. For "we shall make our Heaven where we have sown our purple longings."

THE END

NOTES

NOTES

THE way to read a book is to follow the course one does in eating dinner: first the hors d'œuvres of a foreword; then the soup, fish, entrée, game, salad, and dessert of the main chapters, finally the cheese or savory of the appendix. One should n't attempt to nibble an hors d'œuvres after the roast or try the cheese before the fish. A book should be read with regard for the alimentation of its thoughts. Thus this appendix. The notes contained here are apropos of statements made in the main body of the meal, but it is not necessary to turn back every time one sees a footnote. Leave these notes for a savory.

Note 1. There are two things a man should be fastidious about — picking out a wife and choosing a pipe. Nay, there is a third, she protests — the cleanliness of his cuffs. Cuffs are minor matters, but choosing wives and pipes are serious affairs. Were there space I would write on the twenty-nine desirable points that a man should look for before calculating to propose. The limit of these pages keeps me to pipes.

I prefer three kinds: a long, slim, light pipe, virginally thin; a bit of a short pipe that comes close to my cheek; and a giant affair that fills the palm when you grasp it, like a hearty handshake. The last I smoke in memory of Joyce Kilmer, the poet, to whom it originally belonged. These three I carry regularly with me, bulging out my pockets, which is against domestic regulations and bad for suits. For garden work give me the stub of a clay or a corncob.

One pipe I have smoked constantly at home for seventeen years. My mother (may she be blessed!) presented it to me, saying that pipes were n't half so harmful as cigarettes. After these seventeen years it is still going strong — very strong.

Bulldog pipes I utterly detest; they remind me too much of a Hapsburg jaw. Trick pipes filled with tubes, secret chambers, and patented curves I also dislike. Meerschaums carved into the nether limbs of nude ladies, hunting scenes, and heads of Bismarck are anathema to me.

The great difference between pipes and cigarettes is that the cigarette lacks the remotest possibility of an air of permanence. You can't press it down with your thumb or knock it on your heel or drop it loose into your pocket or rub it on your nose. It does not acquire a sweet aroma after years. You may lose cigarettes by the hundred, but, unless you are accustomed to emotional strains, do not lose your favorite pipe. It is almost as bad as losing your dog.

Being permanent, the pipe can carry with it the heritage of pleasant memories. Whenever I think of my grandfather I recall his study — a stuffy place, sweet with the aroma of old bindings and stale pipes . . . A widow once told me that for many months she kept her husband's bowl of pipes on her desk. Their reek was the most fragrant reminder she had of him — the incense of poignant memory.

A friend from China recently brought me three great, gnarled native pipes, the size of small walking-sticks and with tiny metal bowls holding a pinch of tobacco. In the East they are called "Two puffs and a spit." The Chinese seem to enjoy them, but one marvels how they ever drilled the holes. I smoke mine on the back study porch of evenings or for the amusement of children. They also make effective sticks to throw at strange cats that come marauding around the place. I know of a wooden gatepost in Shanghai that the coolie gatekeeper has drilled out for a pipe. The bowl is in the top of the post. He attaches a reed to the drilled hole and smokes while he calmly leans up against the post in the warm morning sun. I must try that some day.

Note 2. I cannot hold with the Puritan conception of Christ as a sort of deified reformer who did nothing else but cast out devils from street-walkers and drive money-changers from the temple. There are many evidences in the Gospel story witnessing to the social character of Christ, and it is significant that the first miracle recorded was on the occasion of a social festivity — the wedding in Cana. If we are to accept this miracle of changing the water into wine, why not accept the natural surmise that it was good wine, the best createable, full, heady, and joyous wine, wine to warm the cockles of the guests' hearts, and to make them shout uproariously when they flung the old shoes at the departing bride?

By the bye, Richard Crashaw had a delicate explanation of the miracle at Cana in his "Aquæ in Vinum Versæ" —

> Whence in your waters, say, that alien glow?
> What rose newborn your mazed stream hath flushed?
> Some power divine, my guests, confess, is here:
> The modest nymph hath seen her God, and blushed.

Note 3. Theodore Roosevelt, who felt strongly on a great many topics, had decided opinions about Thomas Jefferson. "Not even excepting Buchanan, the most incompetent chief executive we ever had," he described that first Democrat to a friend. (*Theodore Roosevelt and his Time,* vol. II. p. 71.)

Note 4. The plumbline and level are very much overrated instruments when it comes to the restoration of old houses. In many cases the carpenter had better throw them away and depend upon his eye. So long as he can manage to make sash fit and doors close, there is no reason why every line in a restored house should be plumb; in their being out of line often lies their charm.

Note 5. Any gardening library should contain a variety of types of books. They should n't all be bitter practical, as they say in New England; some should be inspirational. In making the following list of forty-eight good gardening-books I have tried to keep this in mind. I do not venture to say that they are the forty-eight best; there doubtless are some lamentable omissions:

Alpine Flowers for Gardens — W. Robinson.
Annuals and Biennials — Gertrude Jekyll.
The Book of Annuals — H. M. Saylor.
Making a Bulb Garden — Grace Tabor.
Color Schemes in the Flower Garden — Gertrude Jekyll.
Color in my Garden — Louise B. Wilder.
Continuous Bloom for Gardens in America — L. Shelton.
Daffodils, Narcissus, and How to Grow Them — A. M. Kirby.
Fertilisers — Edward B. Voorhees.
The American Flower Garden — Neltje Blanchan.
The Practical Flower Garden — Helena R. Ely.
Garden Flowers of Autumn — E. E. Shaw.
Garden Flowers of Spring — E. E. Shaw.
Garden Flowers of Summer — E. E. Shaw.
Our Early Garden Flowers — H. L. Keeler.
The Garden Blue Book — Leicester B. Holland.
Beginner's Garden Book — Allen French.
The Practical Garden Book — C. E. Hunn and L. H. Bailey.
Garden-Making — L. H. Bailey.
The Garden Month by Month — Mabel C. Sedgwick.
The Well-Considered Garden — Mrs. F. King.
Gardens for Small Country Houses — G. Jekyll and L. Weaver.
Old-Time Gardens — Alice M. Earle.
The Greenhouse, Its Flowers and Management — H. H. Thomas.
A Woman's Hardy Garden — Helena R. Ely.
Another Hardy Garden Book — Helena R. Ely.
Hardy Perennials and Old-Fashioned Garden Flowers — J. Wood.
The Herbaceous Garden — Mrs. Martineau.
Home and Garden — Gertrude Jekyll.
Making a Garden with Hotbed and Coldframe — C. H. Miller.
House Plants — Parker T. Barnes.
Manual of Gardening — L. H. Bailey.
Orchids, the Royal Family of Plants — Harriet S. Miner.

The Book of the Peony — Mrs. E. Harding.
Making a Garden of Perennials — W. C. Egan.
The Pruning Book — L. H. Bailey.
Rock and Water Gardens — F. W. Meyer.
The Practical Book of Rose-Growing — G. C. Thomas.
The Rose — H. B. Ellwanger.
The Vegetable Garden — Ida D. Bennett.
Wall and Water Gardens — Gertrude Jekyll.
Wood and Garden — Gertrude Jekyll.
Around the Year in the Garden — F. F. Rockwell.
Pages from a Garden Notebook — Mrs. F. King.
The Rose — J. K. Pemberton.
Studies in Gardening — A. Clutton-Brock.
The Charm of Gardens — Dion Clayton Calthrop.
The Vegetable Garden — Vilmorin-Andrieux.

Note 6. And yet I can sympathize with the newly initiated member of the landed gentry in his search for a name. Giving anything a name is one of the most pesky tasks in the world. Not even naming a baby is a sinecure. Sometime ago the editor of *Vogue* received from a prospective mother the peculiar request for a list of unusual names, male and female, from which she could select one for her prospective child. The lists were assembled and sent — four hundred male and four hundred female — the most amazing array. Not one of them but which, in later life, would have been ample justification for a first-class matricide. I've often wondered which one the anxious, expectant mother chose. She probably fell back on Mary or John.

Note 7. The most monumental prescription for home brew is to be found in William Cobbett's *Cottage Economy*, an exciting little book first published in 1850 and recently re-issued (1916) with a preface by G. K. Chesterton. There are also directions for making bread, keeping cows, pigs, bees, ducks, and rabbits, straw-plaiting, and a memorable diatribe against tea.

Note 8. Sooner or later every man longs for his Sabine

Farm. Lacordaire, the great French preacher of the last
century, was no exception. "I shall never rest satisfied,"
he said once, "till I have three chestnut trees, a potato
garden, a cottage, and a cornfield at the bottom of some
Swiss valley."

Note 9. In her "Figs from Thistles," Edna St. Vincent
Millay has written the almost perfect four lines on this
pleasant time

THE FIRST FIG

My candle burns at both ends,
'T will not last the night.
But ah, my foes, and oh, my friends,
It gives a lovely light.

Note 10. A visit to M. Georges Truffaut's establishment
at Versailles is worth the time of every American garden-
lover going to France. We have nothing like it on this side
of the water, just as we have no rose museums comparable
with L'Hay and the Bagatelle. In addition to a very beautiful rose garden an acre in extent, and a wild garden equally
large, there are the glass houses where M. Truffaut carries
on his soil experiments, working on a new genus each year.
The father of the present M. Truffaut was well known for
his development of the aster. Recently the son has been
experimenting with new soil treatments for clarkia, gera-
niums, and chrysanthemums. In addition to these features
is a large fireproof building that houses his laboratory.
Here a staff of scientists work on soil sterilization and fertili-
zation in one department, and, in another, prepare the life-
history of horticultural pests. M. Truffaut's library of these
pests is extensive. Each volume is bound in glass, so that
the entire story of the pest is revealed. In another part of
the building are the editorial and executive offices of *Jardi-
nage,* a monthly magazine that has a large circulation in

France. During the war M. Truffaut had command of the French, British, and American army war gardens.

Note 11. In *Trivia*, a divine book by Logan Pearsall Smith, this following after beauty is commented on.

"Among all the ugly mugs of the world we see now and then a face made after the divine pattern. Then, a wonderful thing happens to us; the Blue Bird sings, the Golden Splendour shines, and for a queer moment everything seems meaningless save our impulse to follow those fair forms, to follow them to the clear Paradises they promise.

"Plato assures us that these moments are not (as we are apt to think them) mere blurs and delusions of the senses, but divine revelations; that in a lovely face we see imaged, as in a mirror, the Absolute Beauty; — it is Reality, flashing on us in the cave where we dwell amid dim shadows and darkness. Therefore we should follow these fair forms and their shining footsteps will lead us upward to the highest Heaven of Wisdom. The poets, too, keep chanting this great doctrine of Beauty in grave notes to their golden strings. Its music floats up through the skies so sweet, so strange, that the very Angels seem to lean from their stars to listen.

"But O Plato, O Shelley, O Angels of Heaven, what scrapes, what scrapes you get us into!"

Note 12. The Latin of this, found in the Matins of the Feast of St. Agnes in the Roman Breviary, goes as follows —

> Quem cum amavero, casta sum,
> cum tetigero, munda sum,
> cum accipero, virgo sum.

Another part of it has this beautiful lesson — "The Lord hath clothed me with a vesture of wrought gold and adorned me with a necklace of great price. The Lord hath clothed me with the garments of salvation and hath covered me with the robe of joyfulness and hath set on my head a crown as the crown of a bride. He hath put pearls beyond price in my ears and hath cast about me the bright flowers of the eternal springtime."

St. Agnes, so the legend goes, was a young Christian girl whom the Romans tried to force to lead an immoral life. She was martyred for refusing. She has always typified the ideal young virgin.

Note 13. It may make your life happier — it did mine — to learn that in Dorsetshire the native name for yellow stone crop is "Welcome Home, Husband, Though Never So Drunk."

Note 14. The experiences of George Jackman with the clematis, together with the history of that genus as a garden flower up to 1872, is recorded in a book, *The Clematis* by Moore and Jackman, published in 1872. William Robinson, the godfather of present-day English gardening, also wrote a book on the clematis — *The Virgin's Bower*. Although Continental floriculturists made great improvements on the clematis — Lemoine of Nancy, Simon-Louis of Metz, M. Dauvesse of Orleans, and Rinz of Frankfort — none of them did such productive and persistent work as George Jackman in his nurseries at Woking. The Jackmanii race is hardy and gives an abundant summer and autumn flowering.

Note 15. When these pages on "Breakfasting as a Fine Art" first appeared in the *Atlantic Monthly*, I received all manner of correspondence about breakfasts. The most lurid was an attack by an anonymous debutante who accused me of willfully omitting breakfasts in bed among the real enjoyments of life. I am sorry to disagree, but I consider breakfast in bed an abominable habit. Crumbs get in the sheets and scratch your toes. The cream jug upsets. You are so engrossed balancing the contents of your tray that it is utterly impossible to enjoy the meal.

Read in bed? Yes. Sleep in bed? By all means. Be born

and die in a bed? These are preferable. But breakfast in bed — never!

Note 16. When Maurice Hewlett created the character of John Senhouse in *Rest Harrow* and the other two volumes of that trilogy, he conceived a counterpart of our own pioneer orchardist and evangelist, Johnnie Appleseed. Jonathan Chapman was that gentleman's Christian name and he burned with a beautiful zeal to plant frontier orchards. He was born near Springfield, Massachusetts, in 1775, and the first orchard he planted, which can be authenticated, is that of Isaac Stadden, in Licking County, Ohio. He appeared in that part of the country in 1801 with a load of apple seeds in sacks, planting them in favorable spots. In 1806 he drifted down the Ohio River with two canoe-loads of apple seeds lashed together, making for what was then the western frontier. He carried them overland from Fort Duquesne to Detroit. The Indians regarded him as a medicine man and everywhere he was treated with respect. During the War of 1812 he traveled among the Indians unmolested while other white settlers were being slaughtered by these savage allies of Great Britain. In addition to his apple seeds he carried Bibles. He was a religious man, gifted with a native brand of oratory, and he preached to the Indians and settlers *en route*, planted seeds and trees and gave out his Bibles. The record of his travels is one of the most beautifully romantic pages in the history of the settling of our West. It is estimated that in 1838 his seeds had grown into trees bearing fruit over an area of one hundred thousand square miles. When old age approached, he went about visiting his old friends and saying good-bye to them and to his trees.

No one knows what first drove him forth into the wilderness; as he remained a bachelor, it may have been an early love affair, or, maybe — such things being possible — the desire to do good with his apple trees and Bibles. Thus he spent an entire lifetime traveling by foot, boat, and horse on his errands of mercy to the West. The end came in this way — "At the close of a warm day after traveling twenty miles, he entered the home of a citizen in St. Joseph's Township, Allen County, Indiana, ate some bread and milk on the doorstep, read aloud the Beatitudes, slept on the floor, and died in the night."

This Senhousian trait can be marked in another part of the country — in the forget-me-nots that flourish each summer in the meadows of Hingham, Massachusetts. The original plants were brought from France about seventy years ago by a family named Gay, of which Walter Gay, the artist of beautiful interiors, is a descendant. Planted in the meadows, they increased. To-day they are among the glories of Hingham.

I know of no more thoughtful or kindly act than going about the countryside planting seeds. People who like to take long country walks might well slip a packet of wildflower seeds (attainable from any seedsman) into their pockets and plant them as they go along. Imagine the joy of coming back a year or so afterward to find those blossoms flourishing!

Note 17. My ambition to raise columbines was given a gentle prod when, having said to a girl in London that I was doing so, she saucily replied, "I know why. You like their name — columbine. You couldn't dream of specializing on salpiglossis."

Note 18. Yes, it is just as necessary for the woman in Dallas, Texas, to have a house in good taste as the woman in New York City, but I do not hold with the theory that what is good taste in New York would necessarily be good taste in Dallas. I cannot accept good taste as a norm that was established once and for all time and for all men. I do not believe that Divine Providence suddenly descended upon Miss Elsie de Wolfe and Mr. Frank Alvah Parsons and delivered into their hands, the last, only, and final word on what constitutes good taste. Our smart magazines rather suffer from the opinion that the aforesaid Divine Providence did do this thing, and they look to the Atlantic seaboard and New York as the palpitating center of what is correct. The East is inheriting its taste from the Old World. One of these days, from out of the West will come a new taste, and it will be more sincere, more virile, more American. Most of the interiors we see illustrated in our smart magazines exhibit all the form of an old taste and but little of its spirit.

In this same East, the man or woman who does not prefer antiques is looked upon as a parvenu and a little below caste. But why? Is n't most of this rage for antiques a passing fad? Would you wear antique clothes in those antique rooms? These are not wild questions; underneath the taste of any age lies the geographical, religious, and economical problems of that age. Yes, and the sanitary problems, too.

The fad for antiques has gone so far that there is quite a brisk market for books in antique bindings to go into antique bookcases. I know of a New York home where the shelves were filled with old mellow bindings of this sort that gave the room quite a remarkably charming air, but not one of the books would the owners dare open — they were old Greek and Latin tomes!

Note 19. Most of the *Centuries of Meditation* proves very dull reading. It is the typical seventeenth-century pious work, with none of the fascinating stories one finds in William Law's *Serious Call to a Devout and Holy Life*. But, I hold that any book is worth while, if one can cull from it a single sentence that will haunt him through days and weeks. Any amount of ploughing through pietistic phrases is amply repaid when he turns up such a nugget as, "You will never understand the world aright," etc.

Note 20. Did n't she ask me to mark, when I read it to her, this stanza from George Meredith's "Love In A Valley"? —

> Prim little scholars are the flowers of her garden,
>   Trained to stand in rows and asking if they please.
> I might love them well but for loving more the wild ones.
> O my little wild one they tell me more than these.
> You, my wild ones, you tell of honies field rose,
>   Violet, blushing eglantine in life, and, even as they,
> They by the wayside are earnest of your goodness,
> You are of life's, on the banks that line the way.

Note 21. On second thought, I would add some collecting books to that perfect library for the country house. One will naturally put on his shelves such books, of course, as touch on his peculiar collecting hobby, and he can spend a tidy little fortune doing it, too. For a general collector who likes to dally with the antique and curious the following volumes would make a fascinating shelf —

First Steps in Collecting — Grace M. Vallois.
The Pleasures of Collecting — Gardner Teall.
The Lure of the Antique — Walter A. Dyer.
The Practical Book of Period Furniture — H. D. Eberlein and
   Abbot McClure.
Chats on Old Earthenware — Arthur Hayden.
Chats on Cottage and Farmhouse Furniture — Arthur Hayden.
Chats on Pewter — H. J. L. J. Massé.
The Glass Collector — Maciver Percival.
The Earthenware Collector — G. Woolliscroft.
Chats on English China — Arthur Hayden.
Chats on Old Copper and Brass — Fred W. Burgess.
The Arts of Japan — Edward Dillon.
Chinese Art — Stephen W. Bushell.
A Lace Guide for Makers and Collectors — Gertrude Whiting.
Early American Craftsmen — Walter A. Dyer.
Chats on Old Silver — Arthur Hayden.
A B C about Collecting, and *More about Collecting* — Sir James
   Yoxall.

Note 22. To the river in Cochin-China that I hope some day to explore and to that apartment in the Rue du Bac I must add a further ambition which I may — or may never — attain. Namely, serving as butler in some home of the very rich. I have often wanted to understand the moods of a servant, the pompous mood of the doorman, the "Very-well-sir" mood of a second man, the placid and unruffled expression of a beef-faced butler passing dishes.

The servant is just as susceptible to moods as the rest of us mortals, and she has just as much right to them. There must come times when she is ready to slay every member of the family — and with ample justification. The mistress should acknowledge the servant's right to moods.

I know of one household where a Scandinavian servant was installed. Coming from the land of Ibsen, and gloom, her moods were frequent, profound, and significant. Unexpectedly they would descend upon the kitchen and the dining-room, leaving the family terrorized and unfed. Then the mistress gathered up courage and went to her with this proposition: "Olga, you have moods. So have I. You have as much right to your moods as I have to mine. Only don't spring them on us without warning. I am giving you a red flag. When you wake up of a morning and feel moody, hang this in the breakfast-room. We will understand." The red flag was hung out just once. Olga has now been with that family seventeen years.

Trieste

Trieste Publishing has a massive catalogue of classic book titles. Our aim is to provide readers with the highest quality reproductions of fiction and non-fiction literature that has stood the test of time. The many thousands of books in our collection have been sourced from libraries and private collections around the world.

The titles that Trieste Publishing has chosen to be part of the collection have been scanned to simulate the original. Our readers see the books the same way that their first readers did decades or a hundred or more years ago. Books from that period are often spoiled by imperfections that did not exist in the original. Imperfections could be in the form of blurred text, photographs, or missing pages. It is highly unlikely that this would occur with one of our books. Our extensive quality control ensures that the readers of Trieste Publishing's books will be delighted with their purchase. Our staff has thoroughly reviewed every page of all the books in the collection, repairing, or if necessary, rejecting titles that are not of the highest quality. This process ensures that the reader of one of Trieste Publishing's titles receives a volume that faithfully reproduces the original, and to the maximum degree possible, gives them the experience of owning the original work.

We pride ourselves on not only creating a pathway to an extensive reservoir of books of the finest quality, but also providing value to every one of our readers. Generally, Trieste books are purchased singly - on demand, however they may also be purchased in bulk. Readers interested in bulk purchases are invited to contact us directly to enquire about our tailored bulk rates. Email: customerservice@triestepublishing.com

You May Also Like

ISBN: 9780649730179
Paperback: 146 pages
Dimensions: 6.14 x 0.31 x 9.21 inches
Language: eng

Riberside Educational Monographs. The Vocational Guidance of Youth

Meyer Bloomfield & Henry Suzzallo & Paul H. Hanus

ISBN: 9780649663248
Paperback: 196 pages
Dimensions: 6.14 x 0.42 x 9.21 inches
Language: eng

On the Unity and Order of the Epistles of St. Paul to the Churches

Alfred T. Paget

You May Also Like

ISBN: 9780649734504
Paperback: 126 pages
Dimensions: 6.0 x 0.27 x 9.0 inches
Language: eng

The Winston Readers. Primer

Sidney G. Firman & Ethel H. Maltby & Frederick Richardson

ISBN: 9780649653737
Paperback: 180 pages
Dimensions: 6.14 x 0.38 x 9.21 inches
Language: eng

My Class for Jesus: Records of Labour and Success in Sabbath-School Teaching, pp. 1-154

Eliza Mumford & J. Smith Spencer

You May Also Like

A Treatise on Pruning Forest and Ornamental Trees

A. Des Cars

ISBN: 9780649352395
Paperback: 90 pages
Dimensions: 6.14 x 0.19 x 9.21 inches
Language: eng

New Mexico College of Agriculture and Mechanic Arts. Cacti in New Mexico, Bulletin No. 78, May 1911

E. O. Wooton

ISBN: 9780649403158
Paperback: 100 pages
Dimensions: 6.14 x 0.21 x 9.21 inches
Language: eng

You May Also Like

ISBN: 9780649356409
Paperback: 90 pages
Dimensions: 5.25 x 0.19 x 8.0 inches
Language: eng

Constitution and By-laws of the International Garden Club

Various

ISBN: 9780649353576
Paperback: 82 pages
Dimensions: 5.5 x 0.17 x 8.25 inches
Language: eng

Flowers from Foreign Fields

Luella Dowd Smith

Find more of our titles on our website. We have a selection of thousands of titles that will interest you. Please visit

www.triestepublishing.com

Lightning Source UK Ltd.
Milton Keynes UK
UKHW02f0841060818
326818UK00003B/37/P